the ULTIMATE *Another World*
TRIVIA BOOK

the ULTIMATE
Another World
TRIVIA BOOK

GERARD J. WAGGETT

RENAISSANCE BOOKS
Los Angeles

Library of Congress Catalog Card Number: 99-64861

ISBN: 1-58063-081-2

10 9 8 7 6 5 4 3 2 1

Design by Susan Shankin

Cover photo of Victoria Wyndham and Douglass Watson © Robin Platzer, Images; all other cover photos © Barry Morgenstein.

Published by Renaissance Books

Distributed by St. Martin's Press

Manufactured in the United States of America

First Edition

For my editor, Brenda Scott Royce,

who fought so hard for this book

Contents

Quizzes

Acknowledgments

AS EXPRESSED IN MY DEDICATION, my editor Brenda Scott Royce really went to bat for this book. For that, I am incredibly grateful and flattered.

As always, my agents Frank Coffey and Frank Weimann take care of all the business details. Beyond that, they give me the encouragement I need to get through the homestretch and remind me that the occasional misstep is not the end of a career.

Barry Morgenstein and Robin Platz provided the incredible photos used in this book. I thank them as well as Freeman Günther and Patty Carroll from *Soap Opera Weekly* for leading me to them.

I also owe my thanks to my family, which continues to be a source of support for my career: my mother Barbara Waggett, my father Fred Waggett, my brothers Freddy, Michael, and Kevin; my sisters-in-law Keri, Christine, and Julie; my nieces Taylor, Norma, and Ava; my nephew Matthew; my aunt Margaret Connolly; my uncles Eddie and Jackie Connolly; and my cousin Mabel Waggett.

Lauren Harrelson, Rae Costello, and R. Scott Reedy helped me gather the information I needed.

I also need to thank my information source, Eddie Drueding, whose Web site, The *Another World* Home Page (http://www.intranet.ca/~awhp/awhp.html), was an amazing resource. Eddie made himself available to answer all my questions, even the ones whose answers I should have been able to find myself on his site. You can spend hours, maybe even days, going through his synopses, character bios, anecdotes, and other information.

Introduction

TWO WEEKS BEFORE the first draft of this book was due on my editor's desk, *Entertainment Weekly* ran an article pondering the future of daytime dramas. Kristen Baldwin, a staff writer for the magazine, diagnosed *Another World* as a "gravely ill child" and later as a "grande dame that's showing its age." I could not dispute Baldwin's description of the show as gravely ill. Its ratings had dipped below the point where *Search for Tomorrow, Generations,* and *Santa Barbara* had all been cancelled. For years, soap magazines had been announcing each of *AW*'s contract renewals like a stay of execution.

In early April 1999, *Another World* simply ran out of luck. After months of debate over whether to cancel *Another World* or *Sunset Beach*—or both—to make room for *Passions*, a new soap created by former *Days of Our Lives* head writer James E. Reilly, NBC announced that *Another World* would air its last episode on June 25. Although *Another World*'s fans outnumbered *Sunset Beach*'s on the whole, *Sunset Beach* scored higher in the all-important advertising demographic of women eighteen to forty-nine. Another factor that weighed heavily in the decision was that *Sunset Beach* is owned in part by NBC, giving the network a greater share of profits than it received from the Procter & Gamble–owned *Another World*.

In the weeks that followed the cancellation announcement, hope lingered that the show would somehow be salvaged. Fans planned protests, while soap magazines speculated that *Another World* might wind up on another network or in first-run syndication. The Fox, USA, and ABC networks had been mentioned as possible new homes for *Another World*. But in a May 4 interview with TV Guide Online's Jonathan Reiner, Mary Alice Dwyer-Dobbins, who oversees the Procter & Gamble soaps, announced that *Another World* was headed nowhere; the June 25 episode would be its last. Making Dobbins's announcement all the more heartbreaking was the fact that it came on the date of the show's thirty-fifth anniversary.

The cancellation announcement made that milestone bittersweet, to say the least. Yet no one can dispute that thirty-five years is an amazing run for a television show, even a soap opera. Even more impressive, *Another World* had come close to being cancelled during its very first year on the air. Agnes Nixon, who would later launch *One Life to Live* and *All My Children*, saved the show with an intriguing blend of marital rape and murder, which she followed with the show's signature triangle, Rachel/Steve/Alice. That triangle lifted the show all the way to number two in the ratings. Harding Lemay, who took over as head writer three years after Nixon left, would finish the climb Nixon started, bringing the show all the way to number one.

Amidst the constant threats and fears of cancellation that plagued *Another World* since the 1980s, soap fans may have forgotten just how popular this show was during its peak. *Another World* pioneered the way for hour-long soaps, a feat other soap writers claimed could not be achieved. *Another World* was so popular that it launched two spin-offs, *Somerset* and *Texas*. In between, the show's success allowed Lemay and former executive producer Paul Rauch to launch a sister soap, *Lovers and Friends*, later retitled *For Richer, For Poorer*.

Harding Lemay, a playwright by heart with extremely limited soap experience, did more than make the show popular. He blazed a new trail for the daytime drama in the 1970s. He shunned long-accepted soap opera conventions: evil twins, amnesiacs, spouses returning from the presumed dead, and crazed housekeepers poisoning their employers. In his first six years, Lemay continually crafted gripping storylines without resorting to a single murder. (But once he did, one murder followed another.) The major trial for the early part of the decade was the custody battle for Jamie Frame. Instead of adhering to the popular conventions,

Lemay dug for his storyline within each character's history and the interaction between characters.

Daytime, and NBC in particular, have placed too much of their trust in science fiction and the supernatural. Yes, Satanic possession worked miracles on *Days of Our Lives*, rescuing the show from ratings hell. Even more attractive for the sponsors, the majority of new viewers fell within the highly desired demographic of young women. Magic potions, tarot cards, and even a mummy's curse have offered little more than a temporary ratings bump to *Sunset Beach*. The immortal Jordan Stark and his face-morphing key might have driven away some of *Another World's* more traditional fans without picking up an equal number of replacements. It did make perfect sense why NBC would pressure Procter & Gamble, which owns *Another World*, to inject science fiction into the mix. *Days* fans outnumber *AW* fans by nearly two million. Some of those two million who are caught up in Stefano DiMera's latest scheme to change Hope Brady's personality via a satellite might have stuck around to watch *Another World* if they caught sight of Jordan Stark's mind control lab.

Personally, I enjoyed the Jordan Stark storyline. An old fan of the supernatural soap *Dark Shadows*, I miss serialized horror. I also recognize supernatural storylines as ratings stunts. Of course, there is nothing wrong with a soap opera calling some media attention to itself. Back when Agnes Nixon was helming *Another World,* she crossed over Mike Bauer, a popular character from the highly rated *Guiding Light,* to help bring in some of that show's audience. That stunt worked because Mike Bauer fit in with the long-term overhaul she was working on. Unless *Another World* really planned to morph itself into another *Days*—which would have been a mistake—Jordan Stark was only taking the show on a long detour away from a permanent solution.

If the producers and sponsors felt the need to model *Another World* after a successful soap, they should have molded it back into the show it was some twenty years ago. As evidenced by the recent return of Ellen Wheeler, Sandra Ferguson, and Matt Crane, the producers recognized the value of history. More than a few familiar faces needed to be brought back.

The producers also should have brought back that sense of style and mood that separated *Another World* from the other soaps. The characters were in place for such a makeover.

Harding Lemay worked from the tenet that characters did not fall into the extreme categories of sinners and saints; they lived in that gray area in between—an area rich with storyline potential. Many of Bay City's most illustrious residents lived in that gray area. Matriarch Rachel Cory, the show's moral core, was first seen as a cruel and manipulative gold-digger. Vicky Hudson, recently kidnapped by her disturbed sister Marley, used to be the evil twin and Marley the put-upon victim. Jake, the hero who rescued Vicky, raped Marley years ago. Jake's ex-wife Paulina came to town as a con artist and once shot Jake in cold blood. The longtime friendship between Felicia Gallant and Cass Winthrop, a reformed womanizer, began as an adulterous affair. Enough storyline potential lay unearthed in these characters' histories that conflicts did not need to be beamed into town via a time machine.

The right head writer could have done wonders with these multifaceted characters. I thought Michael Malone, who came on board for several months in 1998, was that writer. His own career in daytime resembled Lemay's. Inexperienced with the soap opera formula, both men had been approached about writing for daytime on the basis of books they had written. With Lemay, it was his memoir of growing up in a poor farm family; with Malone, it was his novels, which have been likened to the works of Charles Dickens. With daring tales of homophobia, gang rape, and multiple personality disorder, Malone had transformed *One Life to Live* into the best soap opera on television. I expected him to do the same with *Another World*. Although I admired the rape trial in which police officer Toni Burrell mistakenly accused Nick Hudson of attacking her, other storylines lost focus. The transformation of handyman Bobby Reno into doctor-on-the-lam Shane Roberts felt forced, an obvious attempt to showcase the popularity of actor Robert Kelker-Kelly. Alexander Nikos's vendetta against Carl Hutchins spiraled out of control. Still, given time to better acquaint himself with Bay City and its denizens, Malone, I believe, could have brought *Another World* to new glory days—if not in the ratings, at least in terms of artistic quality.

Unfortunately, NBC and Procter & Gamble were desperately searching for a savior scribe, one who would boost the ratings with every lift of the pen. That desperation led to a dizzying overturn of head writers and executive producers. This decade alone has burned through ten head writers and a half dozen executive producers. That constant turnaround inevitably resulted in uneven storytelling, which in turn drove viewers away, pulled the ratings down, and panicked the sponsors, creating a vicious circle of hirings and firings. From 1971 to 1979, *Another World*'s most successful stretch, it was helmed by the same writer, Lemay, and the same executive producer, Paul Rauch. *Another World* could have learned lessons from *Days of Our Lives*, but not about how to script the realistic exorcism. It needed to learn about patience and stability. James E. Reilly spent years building *Days* to the point where Marlena's possession would light a fire under the ratings. And behind Reilly, there was Ken Corday, executive producer for more than ten years, a position he took over from his mother. No matter how wild the storylines become in Salem, there is a consistency to *Days* that comes from the stability backstage.

Unfortunately, at this point pondering how *Another World* could have been saved is moot. The best we fans can do is to look back upon its history and admire what it accomplished in its thirty-five years on the air. That is what I have tried to do with this book.

World History

I N 1963, *As the World Turns,* which had been daytime's number one ranked soap opera for five years, was hitting the heights of popularity. The show's creator, Irna Phillips, decided to spin off another soap opera from it. In Phillips's original outline, *Another World's* Bay City would be a short drive from Oakdale, the setting for *As the World Turns,* and the Matthews family would be introduced as friends of *ATWT's* Hughes clan. Characters would travel between the two shows. Procter & Gamble, which owned the show, was in favor of the idea, but CBS was already airing six soap operas and didn't have room on its afternoon schedule for another. NBC, however, was looking to beef up its afternoon line-up with soaps. The network was converting its medical anthology show *The Doctors* into a serial format and jumped at the idea of putting on an Irna Phillips soap. Not believing that viewers would switch channels from CBS to NBC, Phillips abandoned all but the most tangential relationship between the two shows.

Another World was co-created by Bill Bell, who had been head-writing *As the World Turns* and would later go on to make *Days of Our Lives* a hit show and create the immensely successful *The Young and the Restless.* Despite bringing three successful soaps to their heights of popularity, Bell was not able to work any magic on *Another World.*

1964: The first episode of *Another World* aired on May 4, from 3:00–3:30 in the afternoon. The show began with a popular soap convention of the day, the death of the family patriarch—in this case, the wealthy William Matthews.

The show opened with the epigraph: "We do not live in this world alone but in a thousand other worlds." *Another World* was one of the few television soaps to open with such an epigraph.

One of the tangential relationships between *As the World Turns* and *Another World* was the character of Mitchell Dru, played by Geoffrey Lumb. Mitchell, a lawyer, had participated in some of *ATWT*'s more notorious trials during the late 1950s and early '60s before moving his practice to Bay City. Prior to *As the World Turns*, Lumb had also played Mitchell on *The Brighter Day*, another Irna Phillips soap. Lumb was the first actor to play the same role on three different soaps.

Phillips had begun *As the World Turns* with a controversial storyline that painted a sympathetic portrait of a mistress (Edith Hughes, played by Ruth Warrick). On that same soap, Phillips and Bell had shocked the audience by having the show's lead vixen, Lisa Miller (Eileen Fulton), gangraped. The pair came up with an equally shocking storyline to kick *Another World* into high gear. Pat Matthews (Beverly Penberthy) got pregnant by her boyfriend, Tom Baxter (Nicholas Pryor), who talked her into having an abortion. The illegal abortion presumably left Pat barren, and she shot and killed Tom. This was the first soap storyline to deal with abortion, a subject of which even primetime television has steered clear.

1965: Micki Grant was hired to play John Randolph's secretary, Peggy Harris Nolan. Although Peggy was originally conceived of as a white woman, Grant won the part, making her the first African American performer signed to a contract role on a soap opera.

1965—66: Despite its occasionally shocking subject matter, *Another World* did not catch on immediately with viewers. Disappointed, Irna Phillips and Bill Bell stepped down from their positions as head writers just after the show's first anniversary. James Lipton stepped in and shifted the focus away from the Matthews family and onto the doctor-centered Gregory family. Lipton left after a few months and was replaced by Agnes Nixon, who had helped Phillips create *As the World Turns*. Nixon killed off the Gregorys in a convenient airplane crash and shifted the emphasis back to the Matthews family.

1966: Movie actress Ann Sheridan, who starred with Ronald Reagan in *King's Row* and with Cary Grant in *I Was a Male War Bride,* came on for a short stint as Katherine Corning, the mother who had given up heroine Missy Palmer (Carol Roux) at birth. Although other film actors, such as Macdonald Carey (DR. TOM HORTON, *Days of Our Lives*), had signed on to headline soaps, Sheridan was one of daytime's first celebrity guest stars.

On June 20, the show switched from black-and-white to color. It also stopped airing live, switching to a videotaped format. With the advent of color, the black-and-white opening credits were traded for a colorized version. Thirty interlocking circles of red, white, blue, and yellow surrounded the title, and the *O*s in the words *ANOTHER* and *WORLD* interlocked.

1966—67: Agnes Nixon imported the characters of lawyer Mike Bauer (Gary Pillar) and his young daughter Hope (Elissa Leeds) from *Guiding Light*, daytime's second most popular soap—and a show Nixon herself head-wrote. This move countered Irna Phillips's conviction that soap audiences would not follow characters from one network to another. (Mitchell Dru, a supporting character transplanted from *The Brighter Day* and *As the World Turns* on CBS to NBC's *Another World*, had never been imagined an audience draw, while Mike Bauer was brought in for a front burner storyline.) In the context of the story, Mike came to Bay City to assist fellow lawyer John Randolph, who had recently been paralyzed. While helping John out, Mike got romantically involved with both John's wife, Pat, and his daughter, Lee.

1967: The character of Rachel Davis (originally played by Robin Strasser) was introduced. Although Rachel Cory Hutchins has evolved into the show's matriarchal heroine, she started out as a much different sort of character. Raised without a father, the insecure Rachel was determined to marry her way into wealth and respect.

1968: The miracle job that Agnes Nixon had done saving *Another World* from cancellation did not go unnoticed. ABC lured her away with the chance to create her own show. Nixon's socially relevant *One Life to Live* was scheduled for the 3:30 time slot, perhaps in the hope that viewers would flip the channel after *Another World*.

**Rachel, past and present
(Robin Strasser and Victoria Wyndham).**

© Robin Platzer, Images

1968–69: A triangle that involved Rachel, the sweet Alice Matthews (Jacqueline Courtney), and a wealthy businessman by the name of Steve Frame (George Reinholt) made *Another World* the second most watched soap on daytime (*As the World Turns* remained number one). *Another World* was, in fact, the first soap to challenge CBS's dominance in the Nielsen ratings.

1969: When Robin Strasser told the producers that she was expecting a child, her pregnancy was incorporated into Rachel's storyline. This was not the first time that an actress's real-life pregnancy was written into the show. That honor belongs to Mary Stuart (JO GARDNER, *Search for Tomorrow*). This was, however, one of the first instances in which a pregnancy was used to complicate a love triangle, a twist that has since become one of daytime's most popular plot conventions.

1970: Due to the immense success of *Another World*, NBC gave Procter & Gamble the go-ahead to spin off another soap opera. Three characters—Sam Lucas (Jordan Charney), his wife Lahoma Vane Lucas (Ann Wedgeworth), and heroine Missy Palmer (Carol Roux)—moved from Bay City to the nearby town of Somerset. The spin-off was titled *Another World: Somerset* while the title of the parent show was expanded to *Another World: Bay City*.

1971: As the ratings for *Another World* dipped, the producers blamed *Somerset*. Robert Cenedella, who had been writing both shows, was told to focus his energy on the spin-off. A few months later, he was replaced there by Henry Slesar, who was penning the popular crime serial *The Edge of Night* at the same time.

Replacing Cenedella at *Another World* was Harding Lemay. Although Lemay's soap opera credits were limited, the playwright's memoir, *Outside Looking In*, convinced the higher-ups that he could take the show in interesting directions.

The series returned to its original short-form title, dropping the *Bay City* tag.

1972: Beverlee McKinsey made her debut, but not as Iris, the character she is most recognized for playing on the show. She first showed up in Bay City as Emma Ordway, one of Steve Frame's sisters. She returned later that year as the manipulative socialite Iris Carrington, who would become the show's signature villainess during the 1970s.

1973: Harding Lemay's storylines were working their magic—*Another World* lured back enough old fans and picked up enough new ones to climb from number six in the ratings all the way to number one, tying for that honor with *As the World Turns* and *Days of Our Lives*.

The Watergate scandal, in which it was revealed that President Richard Nixon had been taping conversations in the Oval Office, made national headlines. Two weeks earlier, *Another World* had aired a storyline in which Iris Carrington (Beverlee McKinsey) bugged her husband's hotel suite. The similarities between the stories prompted the *Wall Street Journal* to print an article comparing the goings-on in Bay City with those in Washington D.C. The article concluded that Iris's machinations made a better story than Nixon's.

1974: On Friday, May 3, the show celebrated its tenth anniversary with a special hour-long episode in which Alice Matthews (Jacqueline Courtney) and Steve Frame (George Reinholt) remarried. Later in the year, Paul Rauch came to Lemay with the news that NBC wanted them to create a new half-hour soap. Instead, Lemay suggested that NBC add on an extra half hour of *Another World* each day.

Prison scenes involving Steve Frame and Rachel's father, Gerald (Walter Matthews), were not taped but rather filmed, a rarity for daytime.

Douglass Watson took over the role of Mac Cory. Although the romance between Mac Cory and Rachel Davis became one of the most endearing in not only the history of the show but of daytime television itself, the writers did not originally bring Mac on for Rachel. After Watson was given the role, the character was elevated from supporting to lead so that Mac could be paired with one of the other leading ladies who were available at the time. However, Victoria Wyndham (who had taken over the role of Rachel in 1972) was so taken with Doug Watson that she flirted with him in their very first scene together. Susan Sullivan, whose Lenore Curtin was one of the characters potentially slated for a romance with Mac, happened to be in executive producer Paul Rauch's office while Wyndham and Watson were taping that first scene. Sullivan noticed the great chemistry between them and suggested they would make an interesting onscreen couple.

1975: On January 6, the show expanded to a full hour, the first daytime soap to do so for more than a special episode. Just as the hour-long anniversary episode in 1974 revolved around a much-anticipated wedding, so too did the first regular hour-long episode. Lenore Curtin (Susan Sullivan) married Robert Delaney (Nicolas Coster). Head writer Harding Lemay had fought hard for this expansion, arguing that he could not write scenes properly unless he was given an hour each day. Former head writer Agnes Nixon told Lemay that he was crazy, she would never write an hour-long soap. Two years later, Nixon's own *All My Children*, like many other day-time soaps, followed *Another World's* lead.

Three fan favorites were let go within a few months of each other. Mary Matthews was killed off with a heart attack because her portrayer, Virginia Dwyer, refused to read the lines she was given. The show's expansion from thirty to sixty minutes gave Harding Lemay the ammunition he needed: If Dwyer couldn't memorize a two-minute scene, he argued, she would never be able to memorize one running six minutes.

When producers could no longer tolerate George Reinholt's fighting on the set and bad-mouthing the show in the press, his character, Steve Frame, was killed in a helicopter crash. Jacqueline Courtney, whose acting style had never appealed to Lemay, was dismissed after she refused to play out a story-line in which a now-widowed Alice adopted Sally Spencer. The role of Alice might have been written out altogether, except that Susan Sullivan, who played Lenore Curtin, announced her own intention to leave. Not wanting to lose two popular heroines in one year, the show recast Alice.

One Life to Live, which was now competing with *Another World* for the 3:30–4:00 time slot, wasted little time hiring both Courtney and Reinholt, who were paired as long-separated lovers. The dismissals of Reinholt and Courtney, considered by many as the stars of the show, paved the way for other shows to fire their own seemingly untouchable troublemakers.

1976—77: On December 31, the *Another World* spin-off *Somerset* aired its last episode. Three days later, NBC premiered *Lovers and Friends*, which had been created by *AW's* head writer, Harding Lemay, and its executive producer, Paul Rauch. (In the planning stages, Lemay had titled the show *Into This House*.) After five months on the air, the show was pulled, revamped, and later returned under the title *For Richer, For Poorer*. During the revamping, Lemay was replaced.

1977—78: In an effort to attract *Another World* fans to check out *For Richer, For Poorer*, Victoria Wyndham and Doug Watson guested on the show as Rachel and Mac. Despite the helping hand, *For Richer, For Poorer* bit the dust on September 29.

1978—79: The 1977–78 season had ended on a high note with *Another World* pulling in as many viewers as the longtime ratings champion, *As the World Turns*. During the 1978–79 season, however, the ratings fell dramatically as the show lost a million viewers. One of the factors cited for the decline was the phenomenal rise in popularity of *General Hospital*, which aired opposite *AW* on ABC. Ironically, *General Hospital's* rise in ratings was due in part to the work of head writer Doug Marland, who had gotten his start writing *Another World* with Harding Lemay.

1979: Despite the show's sagging ratings, executive producer Paul Rauch convinced NBC that the show should be expanded to ninety minutes. (No other soap before or since has had a ninety-minute running time for more than a special episode.) The extra airtime was supposed to allow Lemay, a playwright at heart, to give the show an even greater theatrical feel. From a practical standpoint, the extra half hour would allow the show to begin a half hour earlier than its rival, *General Hospital*. The show expanded to ninety minutes with a shocking episode in which longtime patriarch John Randoph (Michael M. Ryan) was killed in a fire set by his ex-wife, Olive Gordon (Jennifer Leak). (The death was accidental; Olive was trying to rid herself of her new romantic rival, Alice Frame.) After the novelty of a ninety-minute soap opera wore off, viewers lost interest as scenes were dragged out to fill the time slot. Lemay himself was exhausted by the increased workload; he not only plotted the storylines, he also penned four out of five scripts each week. Panicked by the falling ratings, executives suggested that Lemay concentrate on the long-term story breakdowns, and turn the actual script writing over to a staff of five. Lemay, who preferred scripting dialogue to plotting stories, quit.

1980: Though ratings were sagging, Beverlee McKinsey remained popular—so popular that she was spun-off into her own soap opera, *Texas*. *Texas*, it should be noted, was the first soap opera to debut with a one-hour running time. Among the perks in McKinsey's contract, she was given star billing, a rarity for soap actors. To make room for *Texas*, *Another World* was trimmed back to a more manageable sixty minutes and shifted to the 2:00 P.M. time slot.

**The immensely popular Iris Carrington (Beverlee McKinsey)
was spun off into her own serial, *Texas*.**

© *Robin Platzer, Images*

1980–81: The immense popularity of *General Hospital* and *All My Children* on ABC pulled up the ratings of *One Life to Live*, which filled the 2:00 P.M. time slot between them—opposite *Another World* on NBC. Together, the time change, the loss of McKinsey, and the rise of *One Life to Live* cost the show almost two million more viewers.

1981: The opening credits that had been used since 1967 were retired and replaced with high-tech graphics and block lettering. Although the new opening retained the image of the interlocking rings, the Os in ANOTHER and WORLD no longer interlocked.

Harding Lemay published a tell-all memoir, *Eight Years in Another World,* taking readers behind the scenes during his stint as head writer.

1981—82: The writers tried to repeat history by resurrecting the character of Steve Frame. Instead of getting George Reinholt back, the producers hired David Canary, who did not at the time carry the same weight as an actor that he does now. The original Alice, Jacqueline Courtney, was meanwhile enjoying front-burner status on the higher-rated *One Life to Live,* and Victoria Wyndham was well established in the role of Rachel, which had been originated by Robin Strasser. In essence, the writers tried to recreate the Alice/Steve/Rachel triangle without any of the original actors. Unfortunately, the new trio lacked the chemistry that made the original storyline so popular. Viewers also did not take to the revisionist history in which Steve realized that he never really loved Alice and that Rachel was the woman for him. Finally recognizing their errors, the writers killed Steve off again.

1982: Howard E. Rollins joined the cast for a short run as Quinn Harding's (Petronia Paley) brother, Ed. While *Another World* has seen several alumni hit it big in the movies after leaving the soap (including Morgan Freeman, Ray Liotta, and Anne Heche), Rollins was actually up for a Best Supporting Actor Oscar (for *Ragtime*) when he signed on to play Ed.

Hugh Marlowe, who had played Jim Matthews since 1969, died of a heart attack in early May. The following month, it was announced on the show that Jim, who had been vacationing in Europe, had died suddenly in Finland.

For the first time, Bay City was pinpointed to a specific state: Illinois. On her way into town, the character of Julia Shearer (Kyra Sedgwick) mentioned that she was headed to Bay City, Illinois. Prior to this, Bay City had been located ambiguously in the Midwest.

Just as the spin-off *Somerset* aired its last episode on New Year's Eve, so too did the spin-off *Texas*.

1983: Although many popular soap couples marry, divorce, and get remarried, Mac and Rachel tied the knot for a third time, making them one of very few soap couples to go through three legal wedding ceremonies. Mac's son Sandy (Chris Rich) married Rachel's ex-daughter-in-law, Blaine Ewing, in a double ceremony with Mac and Rachel.

Also that year, three of the show's pivotal players were first introduced. January saw the arrival of romance novelist Felicia Gallant, played by Linda Dano, and heiress Donna Love, played by Anna Stuart. At the end of the year, the character of Carl Hutchins (Charles Keating) was introduced as Donna's ex-husband and Felicia's new lover. Because of his hatred of Mac Cory, Carl would evolve into the show's dominant villain over the next three years.

1984: Laura Malone was fired from her role as the vixenish Blaine Ewing for being overweight.

Life imitated art as Harlequin published a romance novel written by Felicia Gallant. In reality, it was co-authored by Linda Dano, who played Felicia, and Rebecca Flanders.

1984—85: The show marked its twentieth anniversary with the return of Jacqueline Courtney as Alice Frame. Courtney had recently been let go from *One Life to Live*. Her return to *Another World* amounted to little more than a publicity stunt. The writers did not come up with a storyline for Alice. A year later, Courtney, who felt that Alice had been turned into nothing more than a sounding board for other characters' problems, left the show.

1986—87: Brittany Peterson Love (Sharon Gabet) went on trial for shooting her husbancd, Peter (Marcus Smythe), who she thought was planning to kill her. The verdict was placed in the hands of a real jury. Ads ran in *TV Guide* and *The Star* inviting fans to sign up for jury duty. Of the 7,500 who responded, fifty were brought into Surrogate Court in

Manhattan where the trial was taped. Of those fifty, seven men and seven women were chosen to serve on the jury. Whereas in an actual criminal trial, a unanimous decision would be required, Brittany's guilt or innocence would be decided by a simple majority. (The writers had scripts prepared for either verdict.) The first vote was split down the middle: The seven men voted guilty, the seven women innocent. One of the men, a lawyer, delivered a speech stating that they had to decide the verdict on the basis of the evidence they had seen in the courtroom, not upon any emotional attachment they had developed for the character of Brittany or any animosity they felt toward Peter. The speech swayed one woman to change her vote to guilty.

1987: A new opening credit sequence was introduced, which featured computer-generated images of various cast members, making *Another World* one of the first soaps to include images of its cast in the opening credits. (Because of the large number and constant turnover of contract players, producers tend to find this practice too costly.) To go along with the credits, a new theme song, "(Another World) You Take Me Away," was recorded by country stars Crystal Gayle and Gary Morris, who appeared on the show as themselves. Gayle and Morris took the duet into the top ten on the country music charts. "(Another World) You Take Me Away" remains one of the very few non-instrumental numbers ever used during the opening credits of a soap opera.

1987—88: The character of AIDS patient Dawn Rollo (Barbara Bush) was introduced, making *Another World* the first daytime soap opera to deal with the AIDS crisis in a front-burner storyline. To ensure maximum viewer sympathy for the character, it was revealed that Dawn was infected not through sexual contact or drug abuse but through a blood transfusion from her mother, a prostitute. Despite being praised for tackling the controversial issue of AIDS, the show was criticized for letting Dawn die offscreen.

1988: On January 6, Brent Collins, who had been playing Wallingford since 1984, died of a heart attack. The following month, Wallingford died as well. Linda Dano, who had been close friends with Collins, counts Wallingford's funeral as one of the most difficult scenes she has ever performed.

The writers went on strike from April until September, delaying the intended return of Harding Lemay as head writer. The strike also postponed Felicia Gallant's wedding to Mitch Blake from the May sweeps until October, when justice could be done to it. The writers hired to fill in for the striking scribes were advised to create short-term stories that could be wrapped up quickly once the strike was over. It was also made known that Lemay wanted Cass Winthrop and Nicole Love to be kept apart until he returned. As a result, a ghost story was initiated in which Cass was haunted by a spirit he believed belonged to his late wife, Kathleen. After the strike ended, Lemay did return, but he stayed only a couple of months.

1989: While most soaps prefer to celebrate Valentine's Day with a grand wedding, *Another World* came up with a different approach to the holiday. In a special two-part episode titled "A Valentine to Singles," the show explored single life in the late 1980s. Ongoing plotlines were placed on hold as Amanda Cory (Sandra Ferguson) and Evan Frame (Charles Grant) spoke to the audience in character about such issues as dining alone, virginity, and fear of commitment. These issues were illustrated with a series of vignettes performed by cast members acting in character.

Douglass Watson (MAC CORY) died on May 1, shortly before the show celebrated its twenty-fifth anniversary. He had not taped any scenes for the anniversary show, which was scheduled for later in the month. Instead, Mac was written out of town on a business trip. The character's death was addressed in June. Mac's funeral, like the anniversary party, brought back a number of former cast members.

Although May 4 marked the show's technical anniversary date, the onscreen celebration began two weeks later. The action spread over a week and centered around a shipboard party, where Cory Publishing was celebrating its own twenty-fifth anniversary. A number of former cast members were brought back, including Jacqueline Courtney (ALICE MATTHEWS), Beverly Penberthy (PAT RANDOLPH), Jane Cameron (NANCY McGOWAN),

The twenty-fifth anniversary brought back such faces from the past as Beverly Penberthy (PAT RANDOLPH), George Reinholt (STEVE FRAME), and Jacqueline Courtney (ALICE MATTHEWS).

© Robin Platzer, Images

Nicolas Coster (ROBERT DELANEY), and Dorothy Lyman (GWEN PARRISH). Christine Jones, who played the murdered Janice Frame, and George Reinholt, who played the twice killed-off Steve Frame, also came back for the anniversary.

1990—91: Jake McKinnon (Tom Eplin) was shot in the spine by a blonde woman. Among the prime suspects were Marley Love (Anne Heche), the ex-wife he had recently raped; Paulina Cantrell (Cali Timmins), whom he had been romancing to get information that she wasn't Mac's daughter; Iris Carrington (Carmen Duncan), who had paid him to spy on Paulina; and a possibly wigged Donna Love (Anna Stuart), with whom he had been having an affair. In an unusual move for a soap opera, the writers left Jake, a major character, hanging in a coma for four months. When he underwent brain surgery, he did have a fantasy sequence, playing poker with all the women who might have shot him. After bringing Jake out of his coma, the writers devoted an entire episode to his mystery. (Few episodes have ever been devoted to one single storyline.) The special episode featured only four actors: Eplin, Timmins, Duncan, and Heche. The mystery ended with an apt twist: Paulina, the shooter, was blackmailed into marriage by Jake, her victim.

1991: Carl Hutchins, who wreaked so much havoc during the early half of the 1980s, came back from the presumed dead. Over the next few years, he would return to Bay City for short stints as actor Charles Keating's schedule allowed. Sometimes those stints lasted only a day or two—but still long enough for Carl to turn a few characters' lives upside down.

Former head writer Donna Swajeski, an admitted MTV fan, wanted to incorporate rock music and videos into the show. Such a move, the producers agreed, could bring in younger viewers in higher numbers. A music video storyline was built around Dean Frame's (Ricky Paull Goldin) romance with Jenna Norris (Alla Korot). A contest was held to find Dean a backup band. Eight hundred tapes were received from rock groups wanting to be on the show. Of those, five were picked to appear on the show. Viewers called in to vote on which band they liked best for Dean. A New

Jersey–based band named Rascal won the honors. The video for "Lady Killer" took twenty-three hours to tape and cost almost as much to produce as an entire episode of the show. Ricky Paull Goldin subsequently guest-hosted NBC's *Friday Night Videos*, which aired "Lady Killer" in its entirety.

Dack Rambo (GRANT HARRISON) made national news when he left *Another World* after learning that he was HIV-positive. He died in 1994. He devoted the final years of his life to AIDS fundraising and awareness, as well as reaching out to those already infected. When Mark Pinter assumed the role of Grant Harrison, the character could often be seen wearing a red AIDS ribbon on the lapel of his suit coats.

1992: Following the practice popularized by primetime dramas, the NBC soaps, including *Another World*, ended each episode with a teaser scene from the following day's installment. After the experiment failed to improve viewership, the practice was dropped.

Three years after its "Valentine to Singles," *Another World* tried something a little more daring for its Valentine's Day episode. A sleeping Cass Winthrop dreamed himself into the shoes of Cass A. Nova, an old-time detective. In the dream, Cass's estranged love, Frankie Frame, became Francesca Kinkead, an ex-girlfriend of Cass A. Nova's who hired him to find a missing piece of jewelry in the shape of a heart. Anna Stuart (DONNA LOVE) became a socialite, David Forsyth (DR. JOHN HUDSON), a doctor in love with Francesca, and Linda Dano (FELICIA GALLANT) a gypsy. Titled "The Case of the Stolen Heart" Cass's dream was filmed in black and white. The symbolism of the missing heart didn't require too much analysis on Cass's part. After waking up, he rushed out to ask Frankie to marry him.

On June 23, the show aired its first and only primetime episode. Earlier that year, NBC had run a special primetime episode of *Days of Our Lives* in the time slot preceding the first primetime airing of the *Soap Opera Digest* Awards. NBC also had the rights to broadcast that year's Daytime Emmys, which had become a primetime special. The network gave *Another World* its shot at primetime in the pre-awards slot. On short notice, a special episode was put together to introduce new fans to the show while also giving longtime watchers something worth seeing. Titled "Summer

Desire," the episode took place on Bay City's hottest night of the year and spotlighted four of the hottest couples: Jake and Paulina (Tom Eplin and Judi Evans); Dean and Jenna (Ricky Paull Goldin and Alla Korot); Cass and Frankie (Stephen Schnetzer and Alice Barrett); and Ryan and Vicky (Paul Michael Valley and Jensen Buchanan). The producers and writers discovered that what could be said, done, and worn (or not worn) in the 8:00 P.M. time slot differed significantly from the afternoon. Although the Emmy broadcast itself pulled in a sizable audience, NBC was disappointed with "Summer Desire," which ranked only number 78 amid all the summer reruns.

1993: Constance Ford, who had been playing Rachel's mother Ada for more than a quarter of a century, died of cancer on February 26. Two months later, Ada died and was given a memorial service in the Cory mansion. Jane Cameron, who had played Ada's daughter Nancy, and Gail Brown, who had played Ada's stepdaughter Clarice, returned for the onscreen memorial.

Following up on "The Case of the Stolen Heart," Cass Winthrop dreamed himself into "Murder on the Honeymoon Express" after finally marrying Frankie Frame. Cast members once again slipped into new characters with the exception of Cass himself and three of his ex-lovers: Cecile de Poulignac, Kathleen McKinnon, and Nicole Love. One by one, the three ladies vanished. In the end, the culprit turned out to be none other than Frankie Frame. As with "The Case of the Stolen Heart," the symbolism was pretty apparent: Frankie had permanently ousted her old rivals from Cass's heart.

1994: On May 4, the show celebrated its thirtieth anniversary with a 1960s-themed party that also celebrated the thirtieth anniversary of Cory Publishing. Although *Another World* began in the mid-1960s, the characters chose their psychedelic party outfits from the late '60s, dressing in headbands, tie-dyed dresses, and Nehru jackets. The episode ended with clips highlighting the romances, adventure stories, and families from the show's history. Although no former cast members showed up for the party,

Irene Dailey, who had not been seen onscreen for a while as Aunt Liz, seemed like a special guest. Although Dailey did not originate the role, Liz Matthews was the only original character remaining on the show, albeit in a recurring role. Dailey got to do some of her Aunt Liz routine, expressing shock at Donna's relationship with the much younger Matt Cory and asking Rachel what her late husband Mac would think about her current relationship with one-time family enemy Carl Hutchins. Aunt Liz has not been seen since that anniversary.

1995: Clips featuring Felicia, Frankie, and Cass were used on the NBC sitcom *Friends*. Rachel Green (Jennifer Aniston) was watching the show while minding Ross's pet monkey. For comic effect, the outlandish background history Rachel was explaining to the monkey had no relation to the characters' real storyline and histories. NBC originally considered using clips from *Days of Our Lives,* but decided against it because Aniston's father, John, worked on the show.

When Robyn Griggs (MAGGIE CORY) got fired, she took her story straight to such tabloid news shows as *Extra* and *Hard Copy*. Contrary to the show's statement that Griggs was being written out in order to take Maggie in a new direction, Griggs maintained that she was fired because of her friendship with John Wayne Bobbitt, who had become a tabloid celebrity after his wife Lorena severed his penis while he slept. Weeks prior to the firing, Griggs claims that she had been warned by higher-ups that her relationship with Bobbitt, which both denied was romantic, was bringing an unwanted sort of publicity to the show. Although show executives declined to comment upon Griggs's accusations, her former co-star Anna Holbrook (SHARLENE FRAME HUDSON) told *Soap Opera Weekly* that the relationship with John Wayne Bobbitt was the last straw in a string of problems concerning the actress.

1996: The immense success of *ER,* the first drama series in ten years to top the Nielsens week after week, gave rise to a number of primetime medical series. Hoping to capitalize on the public's renewed interest in hospitals, *Another World* built new hospital sets and refocused on Bay City

General as the center of storylines. The show also employed the same sort of frenetic camerawork that had become *ER*'s trademark.

The show changed its opening credits again. The Crystal Gayle–Gary Morris duet was dropped in favor of a high-tech instrumental number. The computer-generated graphics were replaced with clips of the show's stars, shot in black-and-white and washed over in varied colors. Much like *ER*, the credits ended with the words *Another World* fading into a lowercase *aw*.

Bay City was plagued by not one but two serial killers. A mercy killer was disconnecting life support machines at Bay City General. The police had barely caught that killer before Dr. Fax Newman killed woman after woman to cover up the sins from his past. Not coincidentally, Maggie DePriest, who had created the Sin Stalker storyline in the late 1980s, had recently returned as head writer. Fans protested not only the senseless decision for Fax to kill off the popular heroine Frankie Frame, but also the particularly brutal manner in which the murder was presented onscreen. After Frankie's murder aired, the writers, directors, and producers began blaming one another for the disturbing way it came out.

Robert Kelker-Kelly, who had recently been fired from his role as Bo Brady on *Days of Our Lives*, returned to *Another World*, where he had played Sam Fowler in the late 1980s to early '90s. Due to his immense popularity on *Days*, the producers overlooked the fact that Kelker-Kelly had walked off *Another World* during his first go-round. Because Kelker-Kelly was not interested in playing Sam again, the character of handyman Bobby Reno was introduced and shoehorned into a relationship with leading lady Jensen Buchanan (VICKY HUDSON). Buchanan's longtime leading man Paul Michael Valley, whose Ryan Harrison had been killed off the year before, returned as a ghost, moving the show closer toward the supernatural realm in which *Days* dallied.

1997: On July 10, *Another World* celebrated Victoria Wyndham's silver anniversary as Rachel Cory Hutchins. It was the first time any soap had so marked a single character's anniversary. Clips from past shows were edited into the present day event of Rachel and her family preparing for the christening of her recently delivered twins. (Rachel's late-in-life pregnancy had

When Robyn Griggs (MAGGIE CORY) was fired,
she took her story to the tabloids. Charles Keating's
(CARL HUTCHINS) dismissal elicited death threats.

© *Barry Morgenstein*

been the subject of much head scratching and debate on the Internet and in the soap magazines.) The anniversary presented a dilemma for the producers. Neither Procter & Gamble nor NBC had saved videotapes of the show prior to 1980. In an effort to include scenes from the '70s, when Wyndham had done some of her best work, the producers issued a request via the Internet for videotapes. Enough footage poured in from fans to allow the show to properly showcase Wyndham's career as Rachel.

1998: Ellen Wheeler returned to the role of Marley Love, which she had originated back in 1984. Marley and her identical twin, Vicky, had been played as a dual role up until 1994, when an overworked Jensen Buchanan made it a condition in her contract that she would play only Vicky. (Buchanan did play Marley for a few days early in the year when Vicky married Jake McKinnon.) Ellen Wheeler, who had been turned down twice when she tried to return as Vicky and Marley, was tapped to bring back the character of Marley alone. A plastic surgery storyline was concocted to explain why Marley no longer resembled Vicky—not that it explained the sudden height difference between the previously identical twins. In an interesting twist, Marley, psychologically scarred from the plastic surgery, was no longer the good twin. By the end of the year, she was kidnapping Vicky to win back her ex—Vicky's current husband, Jake.

Carl Hutchins, whose evolution from signature villain to patriarch made Charles Keating an audience favorite, was written off. Keating's leading lady, Victoria Wyndham, was so physically sickened over his dismissal that she missed a day of work. Angry fans responded to the firing with death threats against then executive producer Charlotte Savitz.

In a year that saw *The Guiding Light* clone its lead heroine, *Another World* journeyed where few soaps had gone before. Mystery man Jordan Stark's arrival in Bay City involved a range of science-fiction staples: time travel (Jordan hails from eighteen-century London), shape shifting (he can morph away the physical deformities in his face with the help of a magical key), and mind control (he hypnotized Matt Cory into marrying Lila Roberts).

April 1999: Only weeks before *Another World* celebrated its thirty-fifth anniversary, word came down from NBC that the show would be cancelled to make way for a new soap opera, *Passions*. For months, the network had debated whether to cancel *Another World* or the lower rated *Sunset Beach*. *Sunset Beach* survived because it, unlike *AW*, was co-owned by NBC, allowing the network a greater share of the profits. *Sunset Beach* has also enjoyed greater resale value in overseas markets.

May 25, 1999: *Another World* taped its final episode. Linda Dano marked the occasion by visiting each of the rooms in the studio—including all of the bathrooms—before leaving the building for the last time. (ABC tried unsuccessfully to buy the rights to Linda Dano's Felicia Gallant character; Dano will instead be reviving the role she played on *One Life to Live* in the late 1970s, Gretel Cummings.)

June 25, 1999: *Another World* aired its final episode, which centered around the marriage of Cass Winthrop and Lila Roberts (Stephen Schnetzer and Lisa Peluso). In homage to Cass's madcap adventures in the 1980s, Cass was kidnapped by an infatuated gorilla shortly before the ceremony. After the final episode, Cass and Lila were transplanted to *As the World Turns,* along with Vicky and Jake (Jensen Buchanan and Tom Eplin). Since *Another World* and *As the World Turns* shared the same time slot in most markets, Procter & Gamble hopes to lure some of *AW*'s disgruntled fans over to *ATWT*. It was a wise move and a fitting end to *Another World,* which was initially conceived as a spin-off of *ATWT*.

Backstage Pass

First Day Memories

From day one, Linda Dano (FELICIA GALLANT) had a powerful fan in her corner at *Another World*. Coming into the studio for her very first day of work, she found a bouquet of flowers waiting for her at the front desk. The card read: "You are the most exciting thing that has ever happened to *AW*," and was signed "Love, Doug Watson" (MAC CORY).

As a good luck charm, Robyn Griggs (MAGGIE CORY) brought her mother to the studio on her first day. She had done the same thing when she landed the role of Stephanie Hobart on *One Life to Live*.

Nadine Stenovitch arrived with a black eye for her first day as Josie Watts Sinclair. When getting into her car that morning, she opened the door too fast and slammed it into her own face.

John Beal appeared in the very first episode of *Another World*, originating the role of Jim Matthews. His first day proved to be his last, as head writer Irna Phillips decided that she didn't like the way he looked on TV.

On Memorizing Lines

Jacqueline Courtney (ALICE FRAME) used to scribble down dialogue on her hands and shirt cuffs.

Linda Dano (FELICIA GALLANT) and Anna Stuart (DONNA LOVE) have both been blessed with photographic memories. They usually need only one or two read-throughs to commit their scripts to memory.

Robyn Griggs (MAGGIE CORY), who used to do her homework to music, memorized her scripts the same way. Not just any music could play in the background while she ran her lines. For everyday scenes, she would only listen to James Taylor. For heavy emotional ones, whether they be romantic or tearful, she needed Celine Dion.

Robert Kelker-Kelly (DR. SHANE ROBERTS) memorized his lines by typing them out.

Nicolas Coster (ROBERT DELANEY) was rehearsing lines with Susan Sullivan (LENORE CURTIN) when she informed him that he had memorized the wrong day's script. Coster had been given three scripts and confused their sequence. He took the script he should have memorized and ripped out pages, which he taped all around the set—on the backs of chairs, in drawers, anywhere he could get away with placing them.

Victoria Wyndham (RACHEL CORY) was instrumental in getting cue cards banned from the set. Back in the 1970s, she complained to then executive producer Paul Rauch that she couldn't stand working with them or with any actors who relied on them.

HAIR, WARDROBE, AND MAKEUP

Sara Cunningham, who originated the role of Liz Matthews, made the mistake of cutting her hair after her first week on the job. Creator Irna Phillips, who didn't like the new look, fired her.

No two twins, even identical ones, are 100 percent alike. So the makeup people came up with a subtle physical differentiation between Anne Heche's Vicky and her Marley. When Heche played Marley, a small mole was pencilled in under her lip. After Jensen Buchanan took over the roles, the mole was dropped.

Tom Eplin's (JAKE MCKINNON) stint in drag presented the makeup department with a small problem: finding fake nails big enough for his man-sized fingers. Ultimately, fake thumbnails were used on all his fingers.

Alice Barrett's (FRANKIE FRAME) hair was dyed red so that Frankie would look a little more like Kathleen McKinnon (Julie Osburn), who had once been the great love of Cass's life.

Stephen Schnetzer credits his current sense of style with playing the well-groomed Cass Winthrop for the past fifteen years. Much of what he knows about fashion he picked up during varied excursions to clothes stores with the show's wardrobe personnel.

Judi Evans Luciano (PAULINA CORY CARLINO) finds one major practical advantage to her character being married. When Paulina is married, Luciano does not need to remove her own engagement and wedding rings before taping and ask stagehands to safeguard them for her.

It took anywhere from an hour to ninety minutes each day to apply the makeup and facial padding that transformed David Andrew MacDonald into the disfigured Jordan Stark.

APPEARANCE IS EVERYTHING

For years, Stephen Schnetzer (CASS WINTHROP) asked the executive producers for permission to grow a beard. That permission was never granted until Cass's wife, Frankie, was murdered. Cass's grief, the producers felt, would justify his sudden change in appearance.

After letting her weight climb to 170 pounds in the early 1990s, Linda Dano (FELICIA GALLANT) turned things around with a diet and exercise program. Her weight loss (forty pounds) fueled the writers' imaginations to do something dramatic with the character. In addition to an on-camera makeover, Felicia also jumped into a passionate affair with the married Dr. John Hudson (David Forsyth).

When playing Scott LaSalle, a character much younger than himself, Hank Cheyne shaved really close.

NEVER WORK WITH ANIMALS . . .

For the scenes in which serial killer Fax Newman (Nick Gregory) left Josie Watts (Amy Carlson) lying unconscious in the sewer, real rats crawled over Carlson's body. While Carlson toughed it out, the scene proved too much for one of the camera operators, who had to leave. A thin layer of chocolate and peanut butter was coated over Carlson's legs, to give the rats an incentive to crawl over and nibble at them. The rats had been raised in a clinical laboratory, so there was no risk of disease should one of those rats have taken more than a nibble.

At the wedding of Felicia Gallant (Linda Dano) and Mitch Blake (William Grey Espy), doves were supposed to be released and fly into the sky. Rather than straight up into the sky, the doves flew into some nearby trees. Crew members shook the trees to try to get the doves out, to no avail.

Initially, Joe Carlino was supposed to have a pet cat, Serpico, named after the famed cop who revealed the corruption in the New York City police department. As it turned out, Joe Barbara, who took on the role of Joe Carlino, is allergic to cats. Serpico, as a result, has been referred to, but never seen onscreen.

the JOYS OF MOTHERHOOD

When Victoria Wyndham's (RACHEL CORY) children were growing up, she refused to let them watch *Another World*. She even fired one nanny who allowed them to tune in.

Alice Barrett's (FRANKIE FRAME) daughter decided to come into the world a little sooner than expected. On the last day before Barrett was scheduled to begin her maternity leave, her water broke. She called up then executive producer Michael Laibson to let him know what was happening, and assured him that she still intended to come in to tape her final scenes. Laibson not only forbade her from coming into the studio, he ordered her to get herself to a hospital. Barrett, who assumed that she had plenty of time, didn't leave for the hospital until hours later. If traffic had been any busier than it was, she might very well have given birth in the backseat of a cab. Her baby arrived just fifteen minutes after Barrett walked through the hospital doors.

When Judi Evans Luciano's (PAULINA CORY CARLINO) baby son Austin, who plays Paulina's son Dante, sees his onscreen father Joe Barbara on the TV set, he calls out, "Joe Daddy Joe," which has taken Luciano's husband and Austin's real-life father, Michael Luciano, aback at times.

Anna Holbrook's daughter Johanna, five years old at the time, was visiting her mother on the set when the opportunity arose for the girl to be an extra on the show. Right before taping was to begin, Johanna decided against it. "I don't want to do this," she told her mother. "I'm not being paid."

SLEEPING ON THE JOB

Before going on live, Joe Gallison (BILL MATTHEWS) would often kick back in his dressing room and review his notes from the dress rehearsal. One day, he dozed off while reviewing those notes and was still sleeping when it came time for him to do his scene. An associate producer had to come to his dressing room and wake him up.

One hospital scene found Sam Lucas (Jordan Charney) lying ill in a hospital bed with Lahoma (Ann Wedgeworth) by his side. During the taping, Charney nodded off. After delivering her line twice without getting a response, Wedgeworth realized Charney was asleep. She surreptitiously woke him up. Charney, who immediately realized where he was, continued on with the scene as if nothing had happened.

During his two years as Hank Kent, Steve Fletcher had one of the longer daily commutes, making the trek back and forth from his home in Albany to the studio in Brooklyn. On the nights when he couldn't handle the commute, he crashed with friends. When that option wasn't available, he spent the night in his dressing room.

Alice Barrett (FRANKIE FRAME), pictured here with Stephen
Schnetzer (CASS WINTHROP), nearly came into work in labor.

© Barry Morgenstein

After the birth of her daughter Julia in 1992, Alice Barrett (FRANKIE FRAME) was barely getting five hours of sleep per night. To compensate, she started napping wherever she could on the set including desktops and hospital gurneys.

GETTING DEEP INTO CHARACTER

Before the day of Michael Hudson's funeral was to be taped, Mark Mortimer (NICK HUDSON), who played Michael's onscreen son, went to Tom Eplin (JAKE MCKINNON) for advice on how to best prepare. Eplin advised him to stay up all night. Mortimer's all-nighter gave him naturally bloodshot eyes and allowed the crying scenes to flow that much more naturally.

Judi Evans Luciano (PAULINA CORY CARLINO) tends to talk a little more quickly than the average person. After daily rehearsals, the production office will often drop her a note, advising her to slow down. Paulina's diet pill addiction actually required Luciano to *speed up* her line delivery. The scenes often required several takes for Luciano to get her diction up to speed. By the time she was done taping, her heart would be racing and her body shaking, almost as if she'd taken some kind of stimulant herself.

The show's stunt coordinator, Jake Turner, did double duty acting as one of Carl Hutchins's henchmen. When Turner's character tried to kill Rachel Cory (Victoria Wyndham), Wyndham performed all her own stunts. She even ran along the catwalk despite suffering a fear of heights. Turner himself got a little too deep into the acting part of his job and forgot about his duties as a stunt coordinator when his character finally got hold of Rachel. Wyndham needed to elbow him as hard as she could to let him know that he was choking her too tightly.

One argument between Alexander Nikos (John Aprea) and Felicia Gallant (Linda Dano) brought real tears to Aprea's eyes. In the context of the scene, Nikos was trying desperately to convince Felicia that he would do whatever was necessary to make their relationship work. As the scene was drawing to a close, Aprea himself started to cry. After the taping had ended, Aprea's eyes were still watering. "I think I went a little too far," he whispered to Dano as they walked off the set.

FREEDOM OF SPEECH

The director had to correct child actor Bobby Doran (JAMIE FRAME) when he repeatedly mispronounced Clarice Hobson's first name "Clorox" (as in the bleach) during rehearsals.

Vince McKinnon (Robert Hogan) ended a bitter confrontation with his long-lost wife Mary (Denise Alexander), who had been living with Reginald

Love during the years she'd been presumed dead, by calling her a "whore." The writers felt that the scene needed the power of that word to make its point, so the producers battled with the censors to allow it to be heard on the air.

Ricky Paull Goldin (DEAN FRAME) wrote the lyrics for the love song that Dean wrote for Jenna. Procter & Gamble then took the song and cleaned it up for the daytime audience. Goldin was amazed at the little things the executives changed. He was told that neither the phrase "God knows" or "Lord knows" was acceptable, but "heaven knows" was.

the PRICE OF FRIENDSHIP

For Christmas one year, Stephen Schnetzer (CASS WINTHROP) wanted to give Brent Collins (WALLINGFORD) Waterford collector martini glasses. Unable to find any at Macy's department store, he instead picked up a Waterford crystal Christmas ornament shaped like a bell, with the year 1987 etched into it. As soon as he arrived at the studio, he told Linda Dano (FELICIA GALLANT) about the gift. Dano, as it turned out, had bought Collins the exact same bell ornament.

Best friends Tom Eplin (JAKE McKINNON) and Chris Bruno (DENNIS WHEELER) loved to play practical jokes on one another on the set. In one of their more popular running gags, they would, as often as possible, pull each other's pants down in front of the cast and crew.

Timothy Gibbs (GARY SINCLAIR) once traded in the first class plane ticket he'd been given to attend the *Soap Opera Digest* Awards for two coach seats so that newcomer Mark Mortimer (NICK HUDSON) could fly out to Los Angeles for the ceremony.

ACCIDENTS WILL HAPPEN

During one especially impassioned love scene with George Reinholt (STEVE FRAME), Jacqueline Courtney (ALICE MATTHEWS) felt the front of her bra come unhooked. Realizing that the camera was not aimed below their shoulders, Courtney continued on with the scene.

During Faith Ford's first week as Julia Shearer, she fell down a flight of stairs when a rug slipped out from underneath her feet. Ford not only stumbled, she fell right on her face. Some good came out of the accident, though. The way Ford handled the fall convinced the producers that she was capable of injecting comedy into her performance.

Ed Fry's first day as Adam Cory pitted him in a staged fight against Robert Lupone (NEAL CORY). During the second take, Lupone's head banged into Fry's nose hard enough to knock Fry out. The crew waited until he regained consciousness, then continued with the scene. Although he felt more than a little out of it, Fry finished up his day's work.

As Robyn Griggs (MAGGIE CORY) has learned, love scenes can be almost as physically hazardous as fight scenes. Her first bedroom scene with Ricky Paull Goldin (DEAN FRAME) required her to crawl across the bed wearing only a teddy. As she did so, her breasts fell out from the top of the teddy. On the second take, suddenly self-conscious about her father watching the scene on TV, she began shaking. During another take, Goldin accidentally bit her finger as she was getting out of the bed.

The first love scene between Lorna Devon and Gabe McNamara (Robin Christopher and John Bolger) nearly ended in disaster. A candle placed in the scene for romantic effect set one of the pillows on fire. The director saw the flames in time to warn the actors and douse the fire before any serious damage was done.

After realizing that Chip Rayburn (David Lee Russek) was the rapist who attacked Toni Burrell (Rhonda Ross Kendrick), Toni and Josie Watts (Amy Carlson) hung him by his feet out of a window to elicit a confession. As Kendrick and Carlson were pulling Russek back in, the radiator by the window was knocked over and landed on Carlson's foot. She escaped with just a nasty bruise on her big toe.

A door through which David Forsyth (DR. JOHN HUDSON) was supposed to make an entrance had been accidentally locked. Forsyth did not realize the door was locked until he rushed to get through it. He not only knocked down the entire wall surrounding the door, he also ripped out the doorjamb.

Tom Eplin (JAKE MCKINNON) was so frustrated with the way one scene went that he punched a wall and broke his hand.

PLAYING INJURED

In the late 1980s, Matt Crane (MATT CORY) was involved in a car accident that left one side of his face scarred. While the scar healed, he did all his scenes in profile.

Rather than keep her facelift a secret, Linda Dano (FELICIA GALLANT) went public in a big way. She announced her upcoming surgery on *Live with Regis and Kathie Lee* and recovered from it on camera. In the course of the storyline, Felicia needed emergency reconstructive surgery after falling through a skylight. Taping that skylight accident was a chore in and of itself for the acrophobic Dano.

Dano was not the first *Another World* actress to recover from plastic surgery on camera. Alexandra Wilson, who played Josie Watts, needed surgery on her nose to repair damage done to it during a childhood accident. To explain the change in Josie's appearance, the writers scripted a storyline in which Josie, an aspiring model at the time, had a nose job. One tabloid newspaper could not separate fiction from reality and published an article stating that Wilson was undergoing plastic surgery purely out of vanity.

Sally Spencer (M. J. MCKINNON) fell eight feet in her own loft shortly before she was to tape scenes depicting M. J.'s prostitute past. Although she could perform some of the scenes, for others, such as M. J. crawling across the bed, a body double was needed. Spencer joked that the painkillers she was taking after the fall helped her get through the taping of some uncomfortably intimate scenes, such as lying on top of a complete stranger.

In one of her wackier schemes, Cecile de Poulignac (Nancy Frangione) kidnapped Cass Winthrop (Stephen Schnetzer) so that he could impregnate her. Their frolic on the beach, filmed on the island of St. Thomas, was torturous for a sunburned Schnetzer. Every time they rolled around, the sand grated across his tender skin.

When Jensen Buchanan taped Vicky's beachside reunion with Ryan (Paul Michael Valley), she was in the early stages of pregnancy and suffering from morning sickness. Between takes, she would run down the beach to throw up.

LIFE IMITATES ART AND VICE VERSA

The way Agnes Nixon wrote about Rachel never having met her father often caused Robin Strasser to wonder just how much Nixon knew about her childhood. Unlike Strasser, whose father died before she could meet him, Rachel did eventually find her father. Strasser found those scenes especially moving and therapeutic to enact.

The various plots revolving around the Cory mansion in the late 1970s required Rachel to spend the majority of her time in the living room. Victoria Wyndham hated the idea that Rachel had nothing better to do with her time than stand around the living room, and requested that Rachel be given some hobby, some justification for being there all the time. The director suggested that Rachel could take up needlepoint. Wyndham opted instead for sculpting even though she herself had never tried it before. Despite her inexperience, she discovered a natural talent for it. Wyndham became such an adept sculptor that she created not only Rachel's pieces, but also pieces that were to have been created by Rachel's teacher. Impressed with her talent, one art collector tracked her down through the show. At first, Wyndham considered the collector merely a fan of the show. As it turned out, he was a well-respected collector and dealer. Several pieces of Wyndham's artwork are on permanent display at the Smithsonian Institute.

Alice Barrett (FRANKIE FRAME) refused to eat a hot dog on camera. Barrett objects to red meat for ecological reasons and has turned down commercials for McDonalds, Wendy's, and Burger King. She told the producers that she'd eat a turkey or chicken hot dog, but not an all beef one. Taking their cue from Barrett, the producers turned Frankie into a vegetarian and had her order a bun filled with sauerkraut.

A practical joker at heart, John Considine (REGINALD LOVE) liked to blur the line between fantasy and reality. He recorded the following message in character on the answering machine at his own house: "You have reached the Love residence. At the sound of the tone, leave your name, number, and three good reasons why I should waste my time calling you back."

Victoria Wyndham (RACHEL CORY HUTCHINS) and her artwork.
© Robin Platzer, Images

Trouble on the Set

WHILE LOVED by the fans for his portrayal of Steve Frame, George Reinholt was not well liked on the set. Actors had threatened to quit rather than work with him. He interrupted not only rehearsals, but tapings as well, to fight about the scripts with producers and directors. He insulted other actors to their faces and spoke about them behind their backs, sometimes while they were within earshot. He accused head writer Harding Lemay of either not understanding Steve (who had not been created by Lemay but by Agnes Nixon) or of deliberately sabotaging the character. When Reinholt didn't like the lines he was given, he mumbled them. His complaints did not stay within the studio walls but traveled to the press as well. Ultimately, executive producer Paul Rauch fired Reinholt. Despite his popularity, his tantrums were preventing other actors from rehearsing their scenes. Lemay suggested that Steve be killed off so that the sponsors would not be able to pressure them into hiring Reinholt back, should the ratings dip after his departure.

Harding Lemay also made an enemy of Irna Phillips, who created the series. When Lemay, who'd never written a soap before, signed on, the much-experienced Phillips was hired as a consultant for him. After months of butting heads, Lemay told the producers that he would not deal with her interference any longer. He was ready to write the show on his own. Although Phillips continued to be paid for the duration of the contract, money was not the issue. She was worried about the Matthews family and what Lemay planned to do to them. Phillips held her grudge against Lemay for years after being fired. At a function hosted by a soap magazine, Phillips publicly embarrassed Lemay, announcing to the crowd that the writing award Lemay won should have gone to executive producer Paul Rauch because he was rewriting all of Lemay's scripts.

Virginia Dwyer (MARY MATTHEWS) not only infuriated Lemay when she rewrote her dialogue, she also frustrated her leading man Hugh Marlowe (JIM MATTHEWS) to no end. After she delivered her own re-worded lines, Marlowe often had no idea what to do with the line he was supposed to say. In his book, *Eight Years in Another World*, Lemay describes Marlowe as "staring at [Dwyer] with overt venom" and Marlowe's feelings toward Dwyer at the end of a scene as "blind, homicidal rage."

After Irene Dailey, an actress who read her lines as written, joined the cast as Aunt Liz, Lemay downplayed Mary and increased Liz's screen time. Whatever information Mary would have been given to relay was now given to Liz. As a result, Dwyer developed a bit of professional jealousy toward Dailey.

Creator Irna Phillips loved Susan Trustman in the role of Pat Matthews. So much so that Phillips gave Trustman more and more to do—more than Trustman could handle. Only a year after she joined the show, an exhausted Trustman begged to be released from her contract. When that request was denied, she turned into a bit of a troublemaker on the set, chewing gum during scenes and employing other tactics to annoy the producers. Trustman's strategy worked. A year later, she was let go.

Constance Ford (ADA HOBSON) became "like a real mother" to onscreen daughter Victoria Wyndham (RACHEL DAVIS) even though the two women started off on the wrong foot with one another. Ford had enjoyed working with Robin Strasser, Wyndham's predecessor, for several years. Ford was so accustomed to Strasser's interpretation that she interrupted her first rehearsal with Wyndham because she disliked the way Wyndham had chosen to play the scene. "Rachel wouldn't do that," Ford told the director. Wyndham took the director aside and informed him that she intended to play Rachel in her own manner. After the scene was taped, Ford apologized to Wyndham for her comment.

Rick Porter (LARRY EWING) hated working with his onscreen wife Gail Brown (CLARICE EWING). Porter, who had dealt with his share of temperamental actresses in his career, thought Brown especially difficult because he found her to be not only unpleasant but unintelligent as well.

Another of the show's popular couples who didn't get along in real life was Sandra Ferguson and Robert Kelker-Kelly, whose characters Amanda Cory and Sam Fowler took on the mantle of the leading young couple in the late 1980s. Just as their onscreen relationship was fraught with problems, so too was their offscreen one. Removed from the pressures of working together every day, the two did manage to become friends when both left the show and moved to California. Ferguson called Kelker-Kelly after he was fired from *Days of Our Lives*, but told *Soap Opera Digest* that she never had an inclination to pick up the phone and get in touch with him after that. She would not get into any further details about the current state of their relationship.

In the late 1980s, Robert Kelker-Kelly inherited George Reinholt's crown as *Another World's* leading troublemaker behind the scenes. He has denied rumors of drug abuse, but has admitted to drinking too much when he was playing Sam. Part of his bad behavior on the set he blames on being too young—twenty-one—when he started working on the show. Additionally, his work in theater had not trained Kelker-Kelly for the rigors of daytime television. "I'd work a fourteen, fifteen hour day, go home and study for five hours, get two hours sleep and go back to work," he told *Soap Opera Digest*. "Sleep deprivation was making me a little bit twisted and my reactions very raw." In 1990, with a few months still left on his contract, he left without warning to straighten out his life. After spending some time in Arizona writing and giving up alcohol, Kelker-Kelly phoned then executive producer Michael Laibson to apologize for his unprofessional behavior and abrupt departure.

Backstage troublemakers George Reinholt (STEVE FRAME) and Robert Kelker-Kelly (SAM FOWLER).

Reinholt photo © Barry Morgenstein / Kelker-Kelly photo © Robin Platzer, Images

For a while, Jenna and Dean (Alla Korot and Ricky Paull Goldin) became the show's hot young couple. Jenna was a convent-raised virgin and Dean a runaway-turned–rock star. In the midst of backstage turmoil (new producers and new head writers), the focus shifted away from Jenna and Dean, leaving the characters floating along with little to do. Korot and Goldin took their frustration and anger about the situation out on each other. For a time, the two, who had once been good friends, could barely speak to one another and dreaded the idea of working together. Eventually, they repaired the friendship.

For the most part, Judi Evans Luciano (PAULINA CORY CARLINO) has gotten along famously with her current leading man Joseph Barbara (JOE CARLINO). Things changed when Luciano was expecting her son, Austin. No matter how nicely Barbara treated Luciano during the pregnancy, she would bark at him to go away and leave her alone, to not even speak to her. Barbara's efforts to talk out their problems only served to heighten the trouble between them. The tension began to affect their work. In one scene in which Joe went to kiss Paulina, Luciano actually pulled away from Barbara. After her baby was born, Luciano apologized profusely to Barbara for the way she acted.

Timothy Gibbs and Amy Carlson took quite a while warming up to one another—much longer than it took their characters, Gary Sinclair and Josie Watts, to become intimate. One of their problems stemmed from Gibbs's practice of discussing ways to improve their scenes with the director, but not with Carlson. At one point, the two stopped speaking to one another except while in character. They had to tape one of their most notorious scenes (Josie and Gary making love in the linen closet) right after they had blown up at each other. Gibbs takes great pride in the fact that viewers could not pick up on the tension between him and Carlson during any of their on-camera moments. The two finally talked through their problems and became good friends.

In late 1989, unhappy with the show, Kevin Carrigan (DEREK DANE) asked to be released from his contract but was refused. Instead, the show used

Onscreen lovers Timothy Gibbs and Amy Carlson (GARY SINCLAIR and JOSIE WATTS) did not always get along so well out of character.

© Barry Morgenstein

him less and less because the producers feared he might walk off the set one day and not return. Nothing he said could convince them otherwise. The following April, he read an article in which his leading lady, Hilary Edson (STACEY WINTHROP), talked about growing tired of the Stacey/Derek storyline. Edson's comments irritated Carrigan so much that he called the magazine and told his side of the story, describing the show's producers and writers as "inept." By the end of May, Derek and Stacey split up (Carrigan considers the break-up his best work on the show), and Carrigan was finally given the release he asked for six months previously.

Like Carrigan, Chris Bruno (DENNIS WHEELER) asked to be let out of his contract when it appeared that the writers had lost interest in his character. The producers declined his request. While Bruno sat around waiting for the show to do something with his character, he missed out on a number of primetime opportunities. Months later, he was called into the producers' office and was told that he was being let go. Bruno was more than a little upset that the show had not let him go when he first asked. As such, he decided not to fulfill the rest of his contract. He finished up work for the day and let the powers-that-be know that he would not be returning. Instead, he headed off to Hollywood, where the producers of *Beverly Hills, 90210* had expressed an interest in meeting with him. *Another World* threatened to take Bruno to court for breach of contract if he didn't fulfill his obligation, but Bruno refused to miss out on another chance at primetime. Nothing evolved from his meeting with *90210*, but no lawsuit was filed against him. The producers simply did not pay him the remainder of the money he would have earned had he finished out his contract. Walking out on the show did not stop Bruno from getting another soap role; two years after leaving *Another World*, he was hired to play gay teacher Michael Delaney on *All My Children*.

All about Rachel

1. What is Rachel's father's name?

   (a) Edgar   (b) Gerald   (c) Charles   (d) Malcolm

2. When Rachel was introduced, what was her job?

   (a) nanny   (b) model   (c) nurse   (d) airline stewardess

3. At what event did Rachel tell Alice that she (Rachel) was pregnant by Steve Frame?

   (a) at Steve and Alice's engagement party

   (b) at Alice's bridal shower

   (c) at Rachel's baby shower

   (d) at the wedding, right before Alice was going to walk down the aisle

4. Iris Carrington lied to her father, Mac, that Rachel had cheated on him with a gigolo named Philip Wainwright. What did Iris present to Mac as evidence, claiming Rachel had used it to pay Philip for his services?

   (a) a ring Mac had given Rachel

   (b) Mac's watch

   (c) Mac's cuff links

   (d) stock in Cory Publishing

5. For whose murder was Rachel sentenced to prison?

   (a) Gil McGowan   (b) Mitch Blake

   (c) Steve Frame   (d) Sven Peterson

6. Where were Steve and Rachel trapped when he realized that he loved her?

   (a) in a mine shaft   (b) on his boat

   (c) in a collapsed building (d) in a bank vault

7. What happened to Rachel in the car accident that claimed Steve Frame's life?

    (a) She was paralyzed from the waist down.

    (b) She was left blind.

    (c) She lost her memory.

    (d) The left half of her face was horribly disfigured.

8. What color was the swan statue that arrived for Rachel after Mac's death?

    (a) red   (b) black   (c) silver   (d) gold

9. Why did Rachel first agree to date Carl Hutchins?

    (a) She didn't know who he was when she met him through the Internet.

    (b) She needed his stock to prevent a corporate takeover.

    (c) She wanted to find incriminating evidence to send him back to prison.

    (d) She was suffering from amnesia.

10. What are the names of Rachel's twins?

    (a) Ada and Cory   (b) Ada and Carl

    (c) Carl and Elizabeth   (d) Cory and Elizabeth

The Greatest Stories Never Told

IN THE LATE 1970s, Michael Randolph (Lionel Johnston) was supposed to come out of the closet after realizing that he was in love with his college roommate. The revelation was going to trigger a break-up between Michael's parents, John and Pat (Hugh Marlowe and Beverly Penberthy)—John would disown his son while Pat stood by the young man. After first giving Harding Lemay the green light, Procter & Gamble killed the story because a plotline about homosexuality could not be resolved the way one about alcoholism could. Lemay was then forced to fall back on a plot device he had not wanted to employ, Michael's sister Marianne (Adrienne Wallace) having a secret abortion, as the catalyst for John and Pat's break-up.

Several years later, after the primetime soap opera *Dynasty* had introduced a gay leading character, the *Another World* writers again considered bringing on a homosexual character, this time in the form of Mac Cory's son, Sandy Alexander (played by Chris Rich). Once again, the higher-ups got cold feet and Sandy's backstory was rewritten. Instead of being gay, Sandy's big secret turned out to be that he had once worked as a male prostitute. Of course, the writers made sure to clearly spell out that he had worked for women only.

The character of Sam Lucas (Jordan Charney) was brought back in the mid-1970s with the intention of eventually pairing him romantically with

Pat Randolph (Beverly Penberthy). After a few weeks, it became apparent that the character, who hadn't been seen in Bay City since the 1960s, did not fit into the new framework of the show. Sam's proposed romance with Pat was shelved and Sam was written off the show.

The character of Gwen Parrish (Dorothy Lyman) was created with the intention of her coming between Mac and Rachel (Douglass Watson and Victoria Wyndham). But Harding Lemay saw such a likable humor in Lyman that he changed his mind about making her the other woman in such a triangle.

After Steve Frame (George Reinholt) went to prison, his wife, Alice (Jacqueline Courtney), was going to suffer a long nervous breakdown. The news that Steve had been transferred to a maximum-security facility was going to send her over the edge. "Over the edge," as head writer Harding Lemay wrote it, was a subdued catatonia. But Courtney interpreted "over the edge" as full-blown hysteria. When she refused to play the breakdown any other way, Lemay gave Alice a much speedier recovery than he had planned.

Irna Phillips came close to killing Alice Matthews (Jacqueline Courtney) during the very first year. Like Lemay, Phillips had grown to dislike Courtney's acting style. Rather than recasting the role, Phillips was planning to have Alice die in an offscreen fire at summer camp. Director Tom Donovan, who had an idea what Phillips was planning, warned Courtney not to move her face so much on camera. Not knowing what else to do, Courtney stood as motionless as she could during her scenes. Although physically uncomfortable for Courtney, that stillness earned Alice a stay of execution.

Like Alice, the character of Rachel was almost killed in the early 1970s. After Robin Strasser left the role, head writer Harding Lemay was disappointed with her replacement, Margaret Impert. Strasser agreed to return for six months so that a more suitable replacement could be found. Fearing that an acceptable substitute would not be found, Lemay seriously considered doing Rachel in. Worthy of the character's stature, her death would have been grand—she would have been either murdered by Steve Frame, trying to protect his marriage, or by Alice in self-defense. While discussing Rachel's possible demise over dinner with the producers, Lemay caught mobsters at a nearby table eavesdropping on the conversation—probably believing the murder plot was real. In the end, Victoria Wyndham's willingness to take on the role saved Rachel's life.

Writer Harding Lemay had originally conceived Iris Carrington's (Beverlee McKinsey) long-lost mother Sylvie Kosloff (Leora Dana) as a Jewish character. Because religion is passed down through the mother, Iris would in turn be Jewish, as would her son Dennis. The network vetoed that particular plot element, claiming that Iris's refusal to accept her mother could be interpreted as anti-Semitic. Lemay had no problem with that, believing anti-Semitism to be a logical extension of Iris's personality. Still the network higher-ups, some of them Jewish, would not allow the plot twist. However, they did allow Lemay to keep the highly ethnic name Sylvie Kosloff, as well as a family history that included a Polish-Russian grandfather who immigrated to America and worked in New York's garment district as a cutter. Dana played Sylvie with a number of typically Jewish mannerisms and voice inflections.

The character of Larry Ewing (Rick Porter) was initially introduced as a future villain for the show. But his sister Blaine (Laura Malone) ended up becoming such a villainess that the writers, much to Porter's dismay, turned Larry moral to counterbalance his sister's wickedness. A disappointed Porter never felt that Larry made as interesting a hero as he would have a villain.

In order to pay off his debt to mobster Tony the Tuna, Cass Winthrop (Stephen Schnetzer) agreed to transform Tony's tomboyish niece Dee (Katie Rich) into a young lady. While Schnetzer enjoyed the harmless flirtation between Cass and Dee, he refused to allow Cass to sleep with Dee. Julie Osburn (KATHLEEN McKINNON), Schnetzer's leading lady at the time, backed him up and the story progressed no further.

At one point, the show hinted that twins Vicky and Marley Love were actually two-thirds of triplets. The third triplet was not going to be a new role for Ellen Wheeler; it was going to turn out to be Scott LaSalle (Hank Cheyne). After being shown a mysterious photo by her father, a mentally unstable Donna Love (Anna Stuart) hugged three pillows to her body and suffered a nervous breakdown. If she could have slept through the birth of her daughter's twin, why not through the birth of a third child as well? That plot was abandoned when Philece Sampler took over the role that Anna Stuart vacated. Sampler looked too young to play Cheyne's mother. (She had a hard time convincing the higher-ups that she looked old enough to play Ellen Wheeler's mother.) Instead, the storyline was revamped into a case of unknown paternity: Was Michael Hudson (Kale Browne) or his brother John (David Forsyth) the twins' father?

During her short stint as head writer in 1988, Sheri Anderson wanted to do a cancer storyline revolving around the character of Felicia Gallant (Linda Dano). Dano was looking forward to playing out such a potentially powerful and challenging storyline. The network killed the idea immediately, afraid that the depressing nature of cancer would alienate viewers.

John and Michael Hudson's (David Forsyth and Kale Browne) mother, Clara (Peggy Small), exhibited the initial symptoms of Alzheimer's Disease, but the story never went any further than that. The storyline and character disappeared from the show soon thereafter. As with Felicia's cancer story, Alzheimer's Disease was more than likely dismissed as too depressing a subject.

With the introduction of Lucas (John Aprea) came an entire storyline revolving around a baby that Felicia had given birth to while still in her teens. At first the writers were not sure who that child would turn out to be. Before it was revealed that Paulina Cantrell (Cali Timmins) was Mac Cory's daughter, the writers planned on making her Felicia's long-lost child. They also toyed with the idea of making Felicia's niece Lisa Grady (Joanna Going) her daughter before ultimately settling on family enemy Lorna Devon (Alicia Coppola).

Jenna's (Alla Korot) real father was never revealed although it was hinted that he was some criminal figure. For a time, the writers planned to make her father none other than Carl Hutchins (Charles Keating).

Felicia Gallant was slated for an interracial romance with her editor, Marshall Lincoln Kramer III (Randy Brooks). While interracial romance was nothing new for daytime television by the 1990s, very few such relationships paired a black man with a white woman. It was far more common to see a black woman paired with a white man. Interracial romance was also not the sort of love story handed to characters well into their forties. After the animosity between the characters had begun to evolve into mutual attraction, the plug was pulled on the story. What kind of backlash their onscreen kiss received was not revealed, but years later a kiss between a young white woman and black man on *The Bold and the Beautiful* resulted in a number of death threats against the actress.

In 1993, Morgan Winthrop (Grayson McCouch) had barely settled into Bay City when he went on trial for the rape of Lorna Devon (Alicia Coppola). All the audience had seen of the rape was a shadowy figure descending upon Lorna. Even Lorna, who was drunk at the time, wasn't certain what had happened. A courtroom admission from Morgan's med school friend Kyle Barkley (Roger Floyd) saved Morgan from prosecution. As originally planned, however, Morgan was indeed supposed to be the rapist. After a period of rehabilitation, he would then emerge as a young leading man. The network and sponsors vetoed the idea, believing that any kind of redemption would take too long, if it happened at all.

After Marlena's Satanic possession lifted *Days of Our Lives'* ratings, other daytime soaps were launching their own tales from the dark side. *Another World* looked ready to follow in *Days'* footsteps when hospital orderly Tomas Rivera (Diego Serrano) was attacked by a patient who claimed to be a vampire. Despite fears to the contrary, Tomas did not turn into one of the undead.

A planned interracial romance between Felicia Gallant
(Linda Dano) and editor Marshall Lincoln Kramer III
(Randy Brooks) was scrapped.

© *Barry Morgenstein*

Inside Jokes

AT THE END of the show's first week, Alice Matthews (Jacqueline Courtney) told her grandmother that her parents and brother Russ had driven to Oakdale (setting for the CBS soap opera *As the World Turns*). Granny Matthews (Vera Allen) asked, "Don't they have some friends who live in Oakdale?" Alice replied, "They know people there, but not friends. . . . " To get this joke, viewers would have had to understand creator Irna Phillips's original plan for *Another World* to be a spin-off from *As the World Turns*. The Matthews family would have been introduced on *ATWT* as longtime friends of the Hughes family. After CBS refused to give *Another World* a time slot, Irna Phillips abandoned the friendship between the Hughes and Matthews families. More than a good-natured joke, some insiders interpreted the line as a sarcastic jab at CBS for ruining what would have been a great idea.

Throughout the first few weeks, Phillips stuck the show's title into the dialogue as often as she could. When talking about Janet Matthews (Liza Chapman), Granny remarked, "She kind of lives in . . . I guess you might say another world." In that same episode, Janet, referring to her own situation, said, "I don't want that . . . so-called woman's world. I've chosen another world to live in." A week later, Pat Randolph (Susan Trustman) commented about Janet, "Someday, she'll find another world, a special world where there'll be a man." And in speaking about his recently widowed mother, Liz Matthews (Sara Cunningham), Bill Matthews (Joe Gallison) said, "She's going to have to make another world for herself."

Throughout the years, the writers would occasionally slip the title into the dialogue. One afternoon, Joe Carlino (Joe Barbara) came home to find his wife Paulina (Judi Evans Luciano) caught up in her soap operas. "Are you all right?" he asked her. "You look like you're in another world."

The joke was not so light when Jake McKinnon (Tom Eplin) argued with Tyrone Montgomery (Henry Simmons), who believed that Jake should forgive Vicky for her ongoing relationship with Shane Roberts. "Everyone knows that she married one man while she was still in love with another," Jake countered. When Tyrone replied that he saw the situation differently, Jake replied, "That's because you're a lawyer. You live in another world."

As a character quirk, Louise Goddard (Anne Meacham) would name each of her plants, often finding inspiration in Greek mythology and literature. Former head writer Harding Lemay chose the Greek names because he and Meacham, longtime friends, had performed a scene together from the Greek tragedy *Agamemnon* in acting class.

Whether intentional or not, the ghost story in which Cass Winthrop (Stephen Schnetzer) was haunted by what he believed to be the spirit of his late wife Kathleen played out like an inside joke on a grand scale. At the time the storyline was initiated, all the contract writers had gone on strike. The show was being penned by ghost writers—writers who didn't want the union finding out that they had broken the strike. Meg Beliveau, associate producer at the time, joked to *Soap Opera Digest*, "It's a ghost story, written by a ghost writer, of course."

The special episode in which newlywed Cass Winthrop (Stephen Schnetzer) dreamed himself into a mystery on board the famed Orient Express allowed the writers to poke good-natured fun at some of the show's storylines, ongoing and past. Ryan Harrison (Paul Michael Valley) had recently discovered that Spencer Harrison (David Hedison) was not his biological father. Cass's dream cast Spencer as a priest, which forced Ryan Harrison's dream counterpart to call him "father" several times. Years earlier, a mysterious statue in the shape of a red swan drew Rachel Cory (Victoria Wyndham) into a much-criticized mystery story. In Cass's dream, Rachel bought a similar red swan and remarked, "It's so ugly, but it speaks to me."

When Charles Keating was recurring on the show in the early 1990s, Carl Hutchins would come to town, stir up some trouble, and escape to parts unknown. After Keating landed a role in the primetime series *Going to Extremes*, Carl was reported to have been spotted in Jamaica, the setting for Keating's short-lived medical series. Incidentally, one of Keating's costars on *Going to Extremes* was Joanna Going (LISA GRADY).

The show has even managed to poke a little fun at its lead-in, *Days of Our Lives,* from time to time. While Vicky (Jensen Buchanan) was touring a beach house she planned to rent for a getaway with Ryan, the real estate agent mistook her for Melissa Reeves, who played Jennifer Deveraux on *Days*, an actress Buchanan herself had been mistaken for on more than one occasion. "I look like a soap actress to you?" an incredulous Vicky asked. The agent then turned her attention back to the beach house, "This is so romantic. It's better than *Days*."

An amnesic Jake McKinnon (Tom Eplin) started worry about his true identity. "What if my name is Dennis and I like to go bowling every Tuesday night?" he asked. "What if I'm an alien? What if I'm like that chick on daytime television who's possessed by the devil?" The chick in question was *Days'* lead heroine, Dr. Marlena Evans (Deidre Hall), whose Satanic possession storyline was the butt of several industry jokes.

The most biting jab at *Days* came from Dr. Shane Roberts (Robert Kelker-Kelly), back when he was living life as handyman Bobby Reno. One of Vicky's sons asked Bobby if he could build a guillotine. Bobby replied, "It would take *Days* to do that." The previous summer, *Days* had featured a scene in which lead hero John Black (Drake Hogestyn) was put into a guillotine. The line had an extra edge of sarcasm coming from the mouth of Robert Kelker-Kelly, who had recently been fired from *Days*.

At one point, Hannah Moore (Jennifer Lien) was bemoaning the trials and tribulations of being in love. "What does it take?" she asked Jake McKinnon.

"You're in love one minute, then two seconds later, somebody else looks better." After listening to her lamentation, Jake asked, "Hannah, where are you getting these ideas? Daytime television?"

During one argument with Cindy (Kim Rhodes), Grant Harrison (Mark Pinter) informed his wife, "I am an ex-senator. I don't play one on TV."

Complaining about her financial state, Sofia Carlino (Dahlia Salem) remarked, "My life may be a soap opera, but I still need to pay the rent."

It's not just the writers who work inside jokes into the script. While Joe Barbara (JOE CARLINO) was starring in *Grease* on Broadway, he made a bet with Tom Eplin (JAKE MCKINNON) that Eplin could not ad lib the word *grease* into all their scenes together. The bet, which lasted throughout Barbara's entire run with the musical, certainly taxed Eplin's creativity, but he did an admirable job, having Jake warn Joe to "keep your greasy hands off me" and "don't start a grease fire" in his restaurant.

Tom Eplin (JAKE MCKINNON) and Jensen Buchanan (VICKY HUDSON) have each poked fun at *Days of Our Lives*.

© *Barry Morgenstein*

Looking for Inspiration

HORDES OF SOAP OPERA vixens through the years have been based to some degree on Erica Kane, played so deftly on *All My Children* for almost thirty years by Susan Lucci. Rachel Cory née Davis, who started off on *Another World* as a scheming gold-digger is one of them. What separates Rachel from daytime's other Erica Klones is the fact that Rachel Davis was introduced to viewers three years *before* Erica. In 1965, writer Agnes Nixon had completed the bible for *All My Children*. After Procter & Gamble optioned the project but passed on it, the bible went into a drawer. Nixon was asked, however, to take on head-writing duties at *Another World*. One of the first characters she introduced to Bay City was Rachel Davis, a scheming model whose destructive relationships with men and obsession with material gain could be traced back to being abandoned by her father.

When Agnes Nixon was creating the character of Steve Frame (George Reinholt), she saw him as a younger version of Cash McCall, the title character in a book by Cameron Hawley and a James Garner film of the late 1950s. McCall was a clever but tough businessman who bought up companies when they were down and sold them for a nice profit.

Once Harding Lemay recognized the comic talents in Dorothy Lyman, he molded her character, Gwen Parrish, into an amalgam of all the madcap heroines that Carole Lombard had played in the movies.

Former head writer Michael Malone never hid the fact that Southern vixen Lila Roberts (Lisa Peluso) was based strongly on both Scarlett O'Hara and

Streetcar Named Desire's Blanche DuBois. Peluso, who counts *Gone with the Wind* as her all-time favorite film, has sometimes wished that the writers would not push the Scarlett connection as strongly as they have. In a scene more than a little reminiscent of the famous movie sequence in which Scarlett rips down the curtains to create a dress to visit Rhett Butler, Lila pulled up a tablecloth to make herself a dress for her first date with the wealthy Matt Cory.

The character of romance novelist Felicia Gallant (Linda Dano) was modeled after Jacqueline Susann, author of such steamy bestsellers as *Valley of the Dolls* and *Once Is Not Enough*. Susann, who died in the 1970s, had been friends with Robert Soderbergh, the head writer who created the character of Felicia Gallant. During Soderbergh's tenure, he would talk to Dano at length about Susann and her passion for living.

The character of Felicia's lover Alexander Nikos (John Aprea) bore more than a passing resemblance to the late Greek shipping tycoon Aristotle Onasis. Nikos was even said to have been married to a famous opera singer. Although Onasis never wed an opera singer, he did have a long-term love affair with world-renowned diva Maria Callas.

In *Misery*, the Stephen King bestseller–turned blockbuster movie, a romance novelist is kidnapped by an overly enthusiastic fan who becomes incensed when she learns that he has killed off the series' beloved heroine. As penance, the fan forces the novelist to write her a new novel. The character of Felicia Gallant was primed to be plugged into a *Misery* rip-off. After her daughter Lorna was raped, Felicia could no longer write romance novels, a decision that didn't sit well with one fan in particular, Walter Trask (Reed Birney). Walter, who had read all her books up to that point, became unhinged at the prospect of never reading another Felicia Gallant romance. So he kidnapped Felicia, locked her in his attic, and forced her to write him a new book.

Felicia had barely escaped from Walter when she and Cass Winthrop found themselves recreating another film. Frank Capra's *Pocketful of*

Miracles cast Bette Davis as the indigent Apple Annie and Glenn Ford as Dave the Dude, a racketeer who turns her into a lady before she meets the daughter she never knew. On *AW*, racketeer Dave the Dude became loan shark Tony the Tuna (George Pentecost), a figure who had been used intermittently through the 1980s and '90s. Like the Bette Davis character, Anne Merriman (Lisa Eichhorn) was nicknamed Apple Annie. Tony called in a favor from Cass and Felicia, asking them to transform Annie into a lady before her daughter Fiona arrived in Bay City. Cass's similar transformation of Tony's niece Dee (Katie Rich) in the mid-1980s was likened to the classic musical *My Fair Lady*.

Film buff Harding Lemay admits to drawing storyline inspiration from the movies he grew up watching. The courtroom scenario of Michael Randolph (Lionel Johnston) defending his mother Pat (Beverly Penberthy) when she was accused of murder came straight from the oft-remade silent film classic *Madame X*.

In 1992, *Guiding Light* received critical praise for the bachelor party of Hampton Speakes (Vince Williams, who played blind musician Dustin Carter on *Another World*). The special episode featured only the male cast members, allowing their characters an opportunity for male bonding. Four years later, shortly before Joe Carlino (Joe Barbara) was to marry Paulina Cory, *Another World* tried the same gimmick for his bachelor party, using only the male cast members for an entire episode. The episode was not nearly as well-received as *Guiding Light*'s had been, due in part to the fact that neither Joe nor many of his party guests had been on the show long enough to merit such attention.

Technically, *Texas* was spun off from *Another World*, but it was launched more on the strength of the CBS serial *Dallas*, then the hottest show in primetime. Head writers Joyce and William Corrington had originally came up with a novel idea for a soap opera tentatively titled *Reunion*, set in the South before the Civil War. NBC wasn't interested in a costly period drama. The network was interested in another *Dallas*. The Corringtons, along with Paul Rauch, didn't even try to hide the inspiration for their new soap, titling it

Texas. Had *Texas* caught on, NBC might have moved it from daytime to primetime, specifically to the Friday night time slot opposite *Dallas*.

In 1991, Anita Hill became a household name when she accused Supreme Court Justice nominee Clarence Thomas of sexual harassment. The Senate's investigation into those charges not only pre-empted soaps for several days, the hearings also fed writers' imaginations. A number of soaps instituted sexual harassment storylines, among them *Another World*. A few months after the Clarence Thomas hearings ended, Dr. Kelsey Harrison (Kaitlin Hopkins) arrived in Bay City. Despite their better judgment, Kelsey and Jamie Frame (Russell Todd) fell into an affair, which prejudiced Jamie against choosing Kelsey for a mentor program at the hospital. Kelsey responded with a lawsuit, and in the fall of 1992, daytime audiences were watching another sexual harassment hearing.

The Game of the Name

THE CHARACTER of Alexander Nikos was originally going to be named Achilles. Head writer Michael Malone thought better of the name after realizing that it would immediately make viewers think of the term *Achilles' heel*, and thus prejudice them to perceive the character as vulnerable. The name Achilles was not dispensed with altogether, it was simply shifted to middle name status.

Prior to returning as Alexander Nikos, John Aprea had played Lucas Castigliano. Lucas's real last name was not revealed until years after the character had first been introduced. The writers felt that having only one name gave the character a certain cachet. At one point, after Lucas asked Iris Carrington (Carmen Duncan) to marry him, she joked that instead of taking her husband's name as was the custom, she would have to drop her own and be known simply as Iris.

Rachel Cory's half-sister, Nancy McGowan (Jane Cameron), was named after Nancy Wickwire, one of the actresses who played Liz Matthews. Wickwire, a good friend of Constance Ford (ADA MCGOWAN), was dying of cancer in 1974 when Ada was giving birth to Nancy. On the show, Nancy McGowan was named after her paternal grandmother.

When the show was having no luck finding a young Latin actor to play Tomas Rivera, the producers decided to Anglicize the role and name the character Jesse. While auditioning "Jesses," the show came upon Diego Serrano, who had been born in Ecuador. He won the role and the character's name went back to Tomas.

When Joe Morton (DR. ABEL MARSH) learned that he would be taking on a dual role as Abel's twin brother, he asked the producers to name the new character Cain so that they could play out a good brother–bad brother storyline. Because Abel's twin was not going to be causing that much trouble, he was given the moniker Leo.

Dawn Rollo (Barbara Bush) was originally going to be named Ivy.

At one point, the audience discovered that the Countess Elena de Poulignac (Christina Pickles) had been born Helen Carter. Her last name was originally going to be Strauss, which the network discarded because it was too ethnic.

Toni Burrell, played by Rhonda Ross Kendrick, was originally going to be called Aisha. She was ultimately given the name Toni after poet-novelist Toni Morrison, author of *Beloved*.

The surname of Toni's boyfriend Chris (Eric Morgan Stuart) went through a couple of changes before the writers ended up with Madison. They also considered the last names Adams and Woods.

Politically ambitious Grant Harrison's (originated by Dack Rambo) name was developed by putting together two presidential last names: Grant as in Ulysses S. Grant and Harrison as in William Henry and Benjamin Harrison, the only grandfather and grandson elected to the presidency. Grant's brother Ryan was given a less stodgy first name because head writer Donna Swajeski wanted to set him apart from his family as the rebel son.

The rebellious Dean Frame (Ricky Paull Goldin) was named for the legendary James Dean, who played the title character in *Rebel without a Cause*.

As originally planned, Joe Carlino was going to be Irish with the last name McConnell. After Joseph Barbara landed the role, Joe became Italian and McConnell was changed to Carlino.

Head writer Donna Swajeski named Paulina Cory (originated by Cali Timmins) partly after her own aunt and partly after supermodel Paulina Porizkova.

The politically ambitious Grant Harrison (Mark Pinter)
was named after three presidents.

© Barry Morgenstein

Cameron Sinclair's (Michael Rodrick) first name was originally going to be Casey.

The character of Ian Rain, played by Julian McMahon, was originally going to be called Carter. Someone pointed out to head writer Peggy Sloane that Carter sounded too similar to Carl, as in Carl Hutchins. The writers could not agree on a new name until the Australian-born McMahon was chosen for the role. At that point, the name Ian just came to them.

Alice Barrett requested that Frankie's daughter be named Charlotte because it was the name of her grandmother, who loved soap operas, especially *Another World*. Just as Mary Frances Frame went by the masculine nickname Frankie, her daughter Charlotte was called Charlie.

ALIASES——CRIMINAL AND OTHERWISE

1. What less-than-glamorous name did Felicia Gallant grow up with?
  (a) Phyllis Gilchrist   (b) Franny Gilland
  (c) Fanny Grady   (d) Frederica Gallows

2. When Rachel was blind, which of her ex-husbands posed as a hospital administrator named John Caldwell in order to win his way back into her heart?
  (a) Mac Cory   (b) Steve Frame
  (c) Ted Clark   (d) Dr. Russ Matthews

3. The mysterious Edward Black, who ran Blackhawk Construction, turned out to be what presumed dead character?
  (a) Carl Hutchins   (b) Reginald Love
  (c) Steve Frame   (d) Mitch Blake

4. What was Reginald Love's avian code name?

(a) The Eagle (b) The Raven (c) The Vulture (d) The Falcon

5. With what first name was Evan Bates née Frame born?

(a) Earl (b) Eli (c) Ellis (d) Edgar

6. When Sharlene Frame was suffering from amnesia, what name did she go by?

(a) Katherine Allen (b) Kate Baker

(c) Casey Churchill (d) Kay Drummond

7. Maggie Cory breezed into town using what cheery alias?

(a) Happy Daniels (b) Joy Lamont

(c) Felicity Child (d) Pleasure O'Rourke

8. What alter ego did Amanda Cory invent to convince her mother, Rachel, that her husband Carl was having an affair?

(a) Taylor Wainwright (b) Genevieve Caldecott

(c) Collette Andrews (d) Hadley Prescott

9. What alias did Marley Hudson invent for herself after undergoing reconstructive surgery on her face?

(a) Mary (b) Marnie (c) Carly (d) Victoria

10. Jordan Stark could morph himself into what alter ego?

(a) David Halliday (b) Joseph Steiner

(c) Steven Roark (d) James Starr

Casting Call

VICTORIA WYNDHAM was not interested in taking over the role of Rachel Davis when the producers first approached her. She had left her role as Charlotte Waring Bauer on *The Guiding Light* to become a full-time mother. Although she needed the income, she didn't like the idea of playing another "black hat." Several meetings with the producers and writers convinced Wyndham that the psychology behind Rachel's wickedness would not go unexamined.

Rumor had it that the role of Rachel had even been offered to Susan Lucci. Ironically, Rachel was based on Erica Kane, the role Lucci plays on *All My Children*.

Doug Watson did not realize what he was getting himself into when he signed on to take over the role of Mac Cory. Having been offered the role without an audition, he thought that he would be appearing for a few days only. When he realized that he had signed on for a full year, he wanted out, but executive producer Paul Rauch wasn't about to let the gifted Watson walk away.

Rue McClanahan earned five dollars as an extra in the early 1970s. She sat at a table during a restaurant scene. In addition to utilizing her as an extra, the producers were also checking out how she came across on tape. Convinced that she looked good, the producers offered her the role of Caroline Johnson, John and Pat Randolph's lunatic nanny.

Neither Victoria Wyndham (RACHEL CORY) nor Douglass Watson (MAC CORY) had been eager to join the show.

© Robin Platzer, Images

Head writer Harding Lemay wanted to give stage actress Anne Meacham the role of Iris's secretary, Louise Goddard, to thank her for participating in so many staged readings of Lemay's plays. Producer Paul Rauch wasn't so ready to hand the role over to Meacham; he had heard rumors that she was difficult to work with. To appease Lemay, Rauch agreed to audition Meacham, along with a number of other actresses he was considering. Lemay not only customized the audition scene to show off Meacham's talents, he also secretly sent her a copy of the scene so that she could be better prepared. After Meacham's audition, Rauch called Lemay to tell him how wonderful she was.

THE ULTIMATE *Another World* TRIVIA BOOK

Nicolas Coster had been playing Robert Delaney on the *Another World* spin-off *Somerset* from its first year on the air. After getting into an argument with the show's producer, Coster ran into Paul Rauch in the hallway. Rauch was executive producing *Another World* at the time. Rauch, who knew about the problem Coster was having, asked if he would be interested in playing Robert Delaney on *Another World*. When Coster said that he would, Rauch worked out the details to get the character transplanted to Bay City.

Susan Keith dropped out of the prestigious Goodman School of Drama in Chicago after *One Life to Live* offered her a three-year contract. Thirteen weeks into that contract, Keith was let go so that the actress who originated Keith's role could return. Because the semester had already begun, Keith could not go back to school. Instead, she spent her time auditioning around New York, and within a month landed the part of Cecile de Poulignac.

Although Linda Dano portrayed Felicia Gallant for years, sixteen, and counting, she didn't want the part when it was first being auditioned. She had recently started a fashion consulting business and wanted to concentrate her energies on running it. Stephen Schnetzer, who had recently joined the show himself and had worked with Dano on *One Life to Live*, insisted that she go in to read. When Dano expressed doubts that she could even play the part, Schnetzer replied, "Are you insane? You *are* this part."

Despite Schnetzer's conviction that Dano was Felicia Gallant, Dano was not the first choice for the role. The producers wanted Jane Elliot, who had won an Emmy playing the spoiled and conniving Tracy Quartermaine on *General Hospital*, and who had recently played a multiple personality role on *Guiding Light*. Elliot declined the role but later expressed interest in joining the cast as Felicia's sister.

Among the actresses who Dano beat out for the role of Felicia was her future castmate Anna Stuart, who joined the cast not long afterward in the role of Donna Love.

The character of Donna Love's father, Reginald, had originally been conceived as British. On the basis of a short stint as C. C. Capwell's brother on *Santa Barbara*, California-born John Considine was invited to audition for the part and won it over the other hopefuls—all of whom had come from England.

Jane Cameron (NANCY McGOWAN) was voted by her fellow acting class students as "Most Likely to Star in a Soap Right out of Drama School." And she did just that. Casting director Liz Woodman was so impressed with a monologue delivered by Cameron at NYU's School of Drama that she convinced producer Allen Potter to screen-test Cameron for the role of Marley Love. Although Cameron was wrong for that part, the producers decided that she would be perfect as Rachel's half-sister Nancy.

Kale Browne landed the role of Michael Hudson mainly on the strength of a screen test he had done for the role of Roman Brady on *Days of Our Lives*. Earlier in his career, Browne hated the idea of winding up on a soap opera so much that he would sabotage his auditions.

The role of Michael Hudson was originally created for Robert Lupone, who was also considered for the role of Peter Love and ended up playing Neal Cory. Michael had been created in part by actress-writer Gillian Spencer, who only months before Michael's introduction had played Lupone's lover on *All My Children*.

When the writers created the character of Marissa LaSalle, who would turn out to be the long presumed dead Mary McKinnon, executive producer John Whitesell wanted a recognizable face in the role, someone with whom the audience would immediately sympathize. Someone suggested Denise Alexander, who had played one of daytime's favorite mothers, Lesley Webber (mother to Genie Francis's Laura) on *General Hospital*. Whitesell offered her the role without even asking for an audition.

Before Robert Hogan's screen-test, the producer gave him a rundown on Vince McKinnon's life history. By the time the producer finished explaining the relationship between Vince and Mary (her being presumed dead for almost twenty years and suffering from amnesia), Hogan broke out laughing.

Sally Spencer was performing in a Los Angeles production of *Cats* when *Another World* was screen-testing the role of M. J. McKinnon. At the risk of breaching her contract, Spencer called in sick so that she could make it to the screen test.

Anne Howard was given short notice to fly from Los Angeles to New York for the Nicole Love audition. Howard was on board a flight to New York before she had even been given a script. On the same flight was Elizabeth Storm, who was also up for the role of Nicole. Unlike Howard, Storm did have a script and, being a good sport, allowed Howard to see it so that she could prepare for the audition. Howard won the role.

Anne Heche (VICKY and MARLEY HUDSON) was approached about working on the soaps after a talent scout from Procter & Gamble spotted her in a high school play. She turned down a role written specifically for her on *As the World Turns* because her brother and father had recently died and she didn't want to leave her mother behind. Years later, after moving to New York, she showed up for the Vicky audition wearing jeans, while the other actresses wore high heels and makeup. Heche believes that her interview, more than the audition, helped convince John Whitesell to cast her as Vicky and Marley. She answered a pair of questions in such different ways that he must have detected a dual personality inside her.

The day before Carmen Duncan headed back to her native Australia after a fruitless year looking for work in the United States, she screen-tested for the role of Iris. Less than a week after she had settled back in Australia, her agent called to tell her that *Another World* had made an offer. Duncan packed up her things and headed back to the States.

Head writer Donna Swajeski created the role of lawyer Byron Pierce for Mitch Longley after she saw a print ad he had done for Ralph Lauren's Polo. It was the model's first professional acting job.

Brian Lane Green tried out for the role of Sam Fowler the first time that it was recast. But as soon as he walked into the audition, he knew that fellow actor Daniel Markel was going to get the job. Two years later, after Markel left, Green went after the role a second time and snagged it. Chris Bruno also tried out for Sam and was cast as Dennis Wheeler instead. Ricky Paull Goldin was deemed too young to play Sam, but the role of Dean Frame was created for him. Amputee actor Jim MacLaren, who played Olivia's physical therapist, David Campbell, first came to the show's attention during the Sam Fowler audition.

After Allison Hossack won the role of Olivia Matthews, she had to prove herself to an even tougher audience: the United States Department of Immigration. The department was hesitant to issue the Canadian-born actress a visa if the job could be performed by an American citizen. Executives from NBC testified that none of the actresses who auditioned in New York, Los Angeles, or Chicago possessed what the producers were looking for.

John P. Whitesell II, executive producer of Another World in the mid- to late 1980s, had known David Forsyth from college. He knew that Forsyth had served in Vietnam as a medic. Along with head writer Maggie DePriest, Whitesell created for Forsyth the role of Vietnam veteran John Hudson, who like Forsyth was coming to terms with what he had gone through during the war. Because Forsyth served as a medical corpsman, whose duties included surgery, DePriest made John a doctor. Forsyth agreed to take on the role as long as he was allowed to have input into the character and the writers didn't portray John as the stereotypical deranged Vietnam vet.

Anna Holbrook and Alexandra Wilson (SHARLENE FRAME and JOSIE WATTS) were cast as mother and daughter even though only five years separate them in age.

Robert Parucha, who had made a name for himself as Matt Miller on *The Young and the Restless*, received a phone call from his friend Russell Todd advising him that *Another World* was looking to recast the part of Jamie Frame. Todd said that he himself wasn't interested in the role but that Parucha should try out for it, so Parucha did. He later heard that Todd landed the part after all.

Although Gerald Anthony (RICK MADISON) left the role of *One Life to Live*'s Marco Dane in 1986, he would occasionally return for short stints. When *One Life* did not jump at the chance to bring him back for a few months in 1991, he told his agent to contact *Another World*. Anthony picked *Another World* because it aired in most markets directly opposite *One Life to Live*.

After running into John Aprea at the *Soap Opera Digest* Awards (he was nominated as Best Primetime Villain for his work on *Knots Landing*), Linda Dano informed him that he would be perfect for the role of Lucas, Felicia's old flame. Aprea and Dano had first met in the early 1970s while working on the short-lived NBC sitcom *The Montefuscos*. Aprea had played Dano's brother, a priest. Aprea's wife, Ninon, was pregnant when Aprea auditioned for the part of Lucas. His agent told him that babies brought good luck. Shortly after Aprea's daughter was born, the show called with an offer.

The audition for Maggie Cory required not only a display of acting ability, but singing as well. Robyn Griggs brought along her then boyfriend, actor-musician Brent Gore, who played a band member in the Saturday morning sitcom *California Dreams*. Brent played guitar while Griggs sang two songs that he had written specifically for her.

When Jensen Buchanan, who left *One Life to Live* in 1990, decided to return to daytime, her first choice was returning to her former role, *OLTL*'s Sarah Gordon. In the time she'd been gone, a new producer unfamiliar with her work had taken over the show. Buchanan's agent sent out feelers about *One Life* bringing Buchanan back, to which the new producer suggested that Buchanan send over tapes of her work on the show. Buchanan took that suggestion as a strong hint that the show was not all that interested in bringing her back. By the time the show decided to resurrect the presumed dead Sarah Gordon and contacted Buchanan, she had already signed with *Another World*.

Buchanan was understandably intimidated when she saw Ellen Wheeler at the audition for Vicky and Marley. Wheeler had not only originated the characters, she had earned an Emmy for her work. She had picked up another Emmy for playing an AIDS patient on *All My Children*. However, the producers decided against Wheeler's return, in good part due to her real-life marriage to Tom Eplin (JAKE MCKINNON). They worried that Wheeler was too associated with Eplin and would prevent viewers from accepting Marley and Vicky's new relationships, namely Ryan and Jamie.

When Buchanan left the show in 1995 with no intention of returning, Ellen Wheeler tried out for the roles once more and was shot down yet again. The producers instead managed to lure Buchanan back. Among the other actresses trying out was Grace Phillips, who had previously replaced Buchanan as Sarah Gordon on *One Life to Live*.

A friend and longtime fan of *Another World* prepared Philece Sampler for the Donna Love audition by filling her in on Donna's history and picking out an outfit that Donna would wear.

While appearing on the Los Angeles–based soap opera *The Bold and the Beautiful*, Colleen Dion appeared in an infomercial for a psychic phone service. The psychic who consulted with Dion predicted that she would have a major upheaval in her life, but that she should not cry about it because she would soon take a trip and sign some documents that would make everything all right. Within two weeks after that psychic reading, Dion was fired from *The Bold and the Beautiful* and traveled to New York, where she signed a contract to play Brett Gardner on *Another World*.

Timothy Gibbs realized that he probably wasn't going to land the role of Joe Carlino when he noticed that every other actor at the audition stood more than six feet tall. He later tried out for the part of Evan Bates with no better luck. The producers and writers liked what they saw, however, and created the role of alcoholic police officer Gary Sinclair for him.

The role of book editor Marshall Lincoln Kramer III (Randy Brooks) was not initially conceived of as African American. The producers were originally interested in Thom Christopher, a white actor who had won an Emmy for playing mobster Carlo Hesser on *One Life to Live*. Christopher, it should be noted, had also been the first choice for the short-term stint of Joe Carlino's father, Eddie.

While waiting to screen-test for Sofia Carlino, Dahlia Salem headed to the bathroom to practice her lines—away from the other actresses vying for the part. By the time she returned to the conference room, she discovered the other four actresses lying on the floor taking naps. (The group had been waiting for hours at this point.) Salem once joked that she won the role because she was able to stay awake during the audition.

Dahlia Salem won the role of Sofia Carlino by staying awake through the audition. Also pictured, left to right: Lisa Brenner (Maggie Cory), Diego Serrano (Tomas Rivera), Kevin McClatchy (Nick Hudson), and Les Brandt (Rafael Santiero).

© *Barry Morgenstein*

John Littlefield had originally signed to play the role of Gary Sinclair's (Timothy Gibbs) shady brother, Cameron. When Gibbs unexpectedly jumped ship to join the cast of *One Life to Live*, the producers decided that Littlefield could play Gary, and they set about finding a new Cameron.

When Amy Carlson announced her intention to leave the show, executive producer Charlotte Savitz worried about finding another Josie. Casting director Jimmy Bohr suggested that Savitz audition Nadine Stenovitch, an actress he had known for several years. Because of her strong physical resemblance to Carlson, Bohr had realized that Stenovitch could not work on *Another World* while Carlson was still there. However, she was ideal to step into the role of Josie. Savitz was impressed not only with the physical resemblance but also the similarity of mannerisms the two actresses shared. Carlson herself described the resemblance as "remarkable."

Kimberly Williams played Steve Martin's daughter in *Father of the Bride*, starred in the short-lived but well-received ABC drama *Relativity*, and flipped greeting cards to check for the Hallmark crown in a number of television commercials. She might very well have been Jenna Norris, too, had she wanted the role. As the character was being developed, Williams was visiting her friend Anna Holbrook (SHARLENE FRAME) on the set. Executive producer Michael Laibson liked Williams's look and suggested that she try out for Jenna. Williams thanked him but declined, stating that she wanted to go to college. She willingly put her college plans on hold, however, when offered a leading role in *Father of the Bride*.

The role of Ben McKinnon attracted a lot of rising daytime stars in the mid-1980s. Auditioning for the role were Jon Hensley, who would go on to play Holden Snyder on *As the World Turns*; Terrell Anthony, who would play Rusty Shayne on *Guiding Light*; and Todd McKee, who would play Ted Capwell on *Santa Barbara*.

Auditioning for the role of Caitlin Ewing were John Wayne's son Ethan, who would play Storm Logan on *The Bold and the Beautiful*, and Jack Wagner, who would play Frisco Jones on *General Hospital* and Dr. Peter Burns on *Melrose Place*. The casting director recognized Wagner's star potential, but by the time he convinced the producers to take a look, Wagner had already signed on with *General Hospital*.

HERE COMES THE BRIDE

1. Which of Mac and Rachel's weddings took place on Valentine's Day?
   (a) first   (b) second   (c) third   (d) all of them

2. Where did Pat Matthews marry John Randolph?
   (a) in her hospital room   (b) in her parents' living room
   (c) at City Hall   (d) in the prison chapel

3. A drunken John Randolph disrupted Steve and Alice's 1974 wedding
   with what allegations against the groom?
   (a) that he had slept with Rachel the night before the wedding
   (b) that he had bankrupted Alice's father Jim
   (c) that he had bribed Rachel's father to commit perjury during the
       custody battle for Jamie
   (d) that he had willingly used substandard concrete in a building that
       collapsed

4. When Marley married Jake, which member of her family caught the
   bouquet?
   (a) her twin sister, Vicky   (b) her mother, Donna
   (c) her aunt, Nicole   (d) her grandfather, Reginald

5. In what unusual venue did Felicia Gallant marry Mitch Blake?
   (a) at the race track
   (b) in a hot air balloon
   (c) in the hospital's emergency room
   (d) at the circus

6. In what foreign city did Cass Winthrop finally and legally marry
   Frankie Frame?
   (a) Paris   (b) Venice   (c) Madrid   (d) Zurich

7. June 12, 1994, the day Rachel and Carl originally picked for their wedding, marked what occasion in Rachel's life?

(a) the fifth anniversary of Mac's death

(b) the first anniversary of her mother's death

(c) the tenth anniversary of the first time Carl kidnapped her

(d) the twentieth anniversary of the day she met Mac

8. How did Sharlene's son Gregory ruin her wedding dress the second time she married John Hudson?

(a) He shrank it in the washing machine.

(b) He colored all over it.

(c) He accidentally set it on fire.

(d) He spilled grape juice on it.

9. Why did Grant and Cindy get married on the street outside the Harbor Club?

(a) A fire had broken out inside during the ceremony.

(b) Donna Love, who bought the club that day, refused them admittance.

(c) The Harbor Club had been shut down as a health hazard.

(d) Vicky had called a bomb threat into the club.

10. Felicia Gallant has been "best man" for what two grooms?

(a) Cass Winthrop and Gary Sinclair

(b) Cass Winthrop and Michael Hudson

(c) Cass Winthrop and Carl Hutchins

(d) Jake McKinnon and Carl Hutchins

Private Lives

FAMILY LIFE

While growing up, Ellen Wheeler (MARLEY and VICKY HUDSON) and her six brothers and sisters helped their parents build the home they lived in.

Robin Strasser (RACHEL CORY) was raised for several years by her grandmother, who won custody after Strasser's mother married a black man.

Judi Evans Luciano (PAULINA CORY) grew up in a circus family. Her father worked the trapeze and occasionally filled in as ringmaster. By the age of two, Luciano had joined the family business as a clown.

Back in high school, Kim Rhodes (CYNTHIA HARRISON) went through a Gothic period, wearing her hair in a Mohawk and shaving it off completely at one point. Her mother responded by telling Rhodes that she would rather they not be seen in public together until her hair grew out.

Whenever a picture of Eric Morgan Stuart (CHRIS MADISON) appears in one of the soap opera magazines, his aunt not only clips it, she also makes photocopies and hands them out to complete strangers.

Kevin McClatchy's (NICK HUDSON) father easily qualifies as one of his most vocal fans and publicists. While driving down the street, McClatchy's father would often roll down his window to encourage passersby to watch his son on *Another World*.

Even after her family moved from Russia to the United States, Alla Korot (JENNA NORRIS) was required to speak her native language in the house.

Judi Evans Luciano (PAULINA CORY) grew up in the circus.
© Barry Morgenstein

Les Brandt (RAFAEL SANTIERO) was born two months prematurely on the kitchen floor after his mother slipped on a green bean and fell.

James Goodwin (KEVIN ANDERSON), who had birthed his share of calves and sheep while growing up on a farm, helped to deliver his second child.

The combination of playing Edmund the Bastard in *King Lear* and giving up smoking made Charles Keating (CARL HUTCHINS) more than a little irritable. Upon finding a pair of sneakers in the kitchen, he threw them into the backyard and admonished his two sons to learn to put their things away. One of his sons pointed out that the sneakers were Keating's own and then offered to buy him a pack of cigarettes.

Naming Names

Born on May 7, 1945 (the day the fighting ended in Europe), Robin Strasser (RACHEL CORY) was given the unusual middle name Victory In Europe.

In grammar school, Linda Dano (FELICIA GALLANT) was nicknamed Willy.

Jensen Buchanan's (VICKY and MARLEY HUDSON) unusual first name was her mother's maiden name.

Robin Christopher's (LORNA DEVON) mother was trying to come up with a name for her newborn daughter when a robin landed on the windowsill outside her hospital room.

Two generations back, Joe Barbara's (JOE CARLINO) family name was spelled Barbar*o*. A government official mistook the *o* for an *a* and officially changed the last name.

Dondre Whitfield's (JESSE LAWRENCE) mother initially intended to name her son André. Deciding the name had become too common, she played around with it until she came up with the unusual variation Dondre.

Ricky Paull Goldin's (DEAN FRAME) football team nicknamed him "Hollywood" because his acting jobs forced him to miss so many games and practices.

It is a tradition in Carmen Duncan's (IRIS CARRINGTON) family for one of the children to be given his or her mother's maiden name as a first name. Duncan's mother's was Margaret Carmen; her son is named Duncan Barrett.

Physical Attributes

Charles Keating's (CARL HUTCHINS) hair started turning gray when he was only sixteen years old.

Jensen Buchanan (VICKY and MARLEY HUDSON) was once forty pounds overweight.

In her battles to keep her weight down, former model Linda Dano (FELICIA GALLANT) suffered through a period of bulimia, a fact she revealed while taping an episode on the subject for her talk show *Attitudes*.

Many of Mark Mortimer's (NICK HUDSON) classmates didn't recognize him when he attended his high school reunion. He had grown eleven inches taller and gained seventy pounds after graduation.

Grayson McCouch (MORGAN WINTHROP) did not start talking until he was five years old.

Brian Lane Green (SAM FOWLER) stuttered as a child, but the speech impediment disappeared when he sang.

Jim MacLaren (DAVID CAMPBELL) lost his leg as a result of a bus accident. While in the hospital immediately after the accident, MacLaren was pronounced dead not once but twice.

Two heart attacks in 1985 forced Gerald Anthony (RICK MADISON) to give up drinking and smoking.

Patti D'Arbanville (CHRISTY CARSON) was hooked on heroin for three years. She didn't break the habit until a friend locked her inside her apartment for a week.

EDUCATION

Robert Kelker-Kelly (SAM FOWLER and DR. SHANE ROBERTS) was kicked out of high school after hitting the dean of students.

Victoria Wyndham (RACHEL CORY) ruined her opportunity to attend Sarah Lawrence, her only college choice, by revealing during the interview that she didn't intend to stick around for the full four years.

Joe Barbara (JOE CARLINO) had an extra reason for not wanting to get sent to the principal's office in grammar school—his mother was the principal's secretary.

Anne Heche (VICKY and MARLEY HUDSON) went to the same high school from which film actresses Darryl Hannah (*Splash*) and Jennifer Beals (*Flashdance*) graduated.

As the son of a former prime minister, Julian McMahon (IAN RAIN) was chauffeured to school in a Rolls Royce every day until he insisted upon riding the bus with the other schoolchildren.

The head of the musical theater department at Carnegie Mellon advised Kaitlin Hopkins (DR. KELSEY HARRISON) to steer clear of singing and concentrate solely upon acting. After her singing voice received a positive review in the *Los Angeles Times*, Hopkins mailed a copy of the article to the department head.

Nadine Stenovitch (JOSIE WATTS) studied acting at Boston University with Cynthia Watros, who won an Emmy as demented nurse Annie Dutton on *Guiding Light* and subbed for Jensen Buchanan as Vicky Hudson McKinnon.

Charles Grant (EVAN BATES) graduated from college at age nineteen.

Alicia Coppola (LORNA DEVON) was a year ahead of Grayson McCouch (DR. MORGAN WINTHROP) at their prep school in Kent, Connecticut. They would have been in the same class had McCouch not been kept back a year in the fourth grade.

Grayson McCouch and Bronson Pickett (SCOTT GUTHRIE) were classmates at Hamilton College in New York. Pickett was torn between majoring in theater and physics.

Robin Strasser (RACHEL DAVIS) was accepted into the graduate drama program at Yale straight out of high school.

Kathleen Widdoes (ROSE PERRINI) won a Fulbright scholarship to study at the Sorbonne in Paris.

John Considine (VIC HASTINGS and REGINALD LOVE) graduated from UCLA as a member of the Phi Beta Kappa fraternity.

Chris Bruno (DENNIS WHEELER) dropped out of prep school. While attending public school, he fell in with the wrong crowd. Realizing that he needed to get his life back on track, he asked to be readmitted to the prep school. The headmaster agreed under the conditions that Bruno attend summer school and sign up for three sports teams (football, baseball, and wrestling) during the school year.

Vice President Dan Quayle's visit to Robyn Griggs's (MAGGIE CORY) high school made national news when one of her fellow students gave Quayle the middle finger.

RELIGION

A Mormon, Ellen Wheeler (VICKY and MARLEY LOVE) does not drink, smoke, or swear.

Judith Barcroft (LENORE CURTIN) was the daughter of a minister. Her father, Reverend James Williams, played the minister who married Lenore to Walter Curtin.

While growing up, Linda Dano (FELICIA GALLANT) used to conduct Bible classes for the younger children in her neighborhood.

Raised by a Quaker father and an Israeli mother, Grayson McCouch's (MORGAN WINTHROP) own religious beliefs lean toward Judaism.

Michael M. Ryan (JOHN RANDOLPH) is a lector at his church and has served on the parish council.

As a child, Marcia McCabe, who played assassin Bunny Eberhardt, used to sing in the church choir.

Brian Lane Green (SAM FOWLER) is descended from a long line of preachers (including his great-grandmother) and was expected to follow in their footsteps.

MILITARY EXPERIENCE

Douglass Watson (MAC CORY) earned two Purple Hearts and a Distinguished Flying Cross during his World War II Air Force career.

Charles Keating (CARL HUTCHINS), who was going to be an artillery gunner during the early years of the Vietnam War, would occasionally sleepwalk through his barracks, shouting out, "I won't kill him! I won't kill him."

David Canary's (STEVE FRAME) Broadway career was interrupted after he was drafted. He continued performing in the service, however, and was named Best Popular Singer in an All Army Entertainment Competition.

Nicolas Coster (ROBERT DELANEY) is a licensed skipper with the United States Coast Guard. He is also a licensed scuba instructor.

The son of an attack fighter pilot and a navy nurse, David Forsyth (DR. JOHN HUDSON) was a medic in the Vietnam War.

Mark Pinter (GRANT HARRISON) came dangerously close to being drafted into the Vietnam War after he graduated from college. His lottery number was quite low, and he just barely missed the cut off.

The blue lightning bolt tattoos on Mark Mortimer's (NICK HUDSON) shoulders were designed after the symbols he wore on his Army uniform. He was honorably discharged from the Army after stealing a jeep to take a ride to the beach one night.

UNUSUAL SHOW BUSINESS JOBS

Victoria Wyndham (RACHEL CORY) used to perform improvisational satire with noted comedienne Lily Tomlin. Wyndham was able to observe Tomlin create and work on one of her most famous characters, Ernestine the telephone operator.

Beverlee McKinsey (IRIS CARRINGTON) used to host a local children's show in Boston.

Alicia Coppola (LORNA DEVON) co-hosted the TV trivia-themed game show *Remote Control* on MTV.

As a child actor, Ariana Chase (MARIANNE RANDOLPH) was one of the original cast members on *Sesame Street*. She was a little frightened by the Muppets, Big Bird in particular.

Anne Heche (VICKY and MARLEY HUDSON) made an anti-drug film aimed at children, which also starred Ernie, the Keebler Elf.

As Miss Golden Globe, Kaitlin Hopkins (DR. KELSEY HARRISON) passed out the awards to the winners at the Golden Globe ceremony.

After sending his headshot off to an agent, sixteen-year-old Diego Serrano (TOMAS RIVERA) found himself appearing in Gloria Estefan's "Seal Our Fate" video, which led to another video for a song by Spanish-language singer Naomi. Producers from *Telemusica* (the Latin American version of MTV), which was doing a behind-the-scenes report on the video, eventually hired him as an on-air personality.

Robert Kelker-Kelly (SAM FOWLER and DR. SHANE ROBERTS) once barked off-stage like a small dog as the sound effect for a play.

MODELING GIGS

At the age of four months, Lisa Peluso (LILA ROBERTS) was chosen to be "caption baby" for the Philadelphia Phillies, appearing in a number of print ads for the baseball team. By the age of five, she was working in television commercials; she has made more than one hundred to date.

Painted images of Robin Christopher (LORNA DEVON) and her long flowing red hair have graced the covers of several romance novels.

Mark Mortimer (NICK HUDSON) has modeled underwear in television commercials, and his image is still being used on the packages.

As a model, Ed Fry (ADAM CORY) made it clear to his agents that he would not pose in his underwear, nor would he promote alcohol or cigarettes.

Hank Cheyne (SCOTT LASALLE) did a photo session with supermodel Christie Brinkley for Italian *Vogue*.

Alicia Coppola (LORNA DEVON) modeled clothes on Linda Dano's talk show *Attitudes* but didn't get a chance at the time to meet her future "mother."

The character of Esmerelda in Disney's animated film *The Hunchback of Notre Dame* was modeled after Alla Korot (JENNA NORRIS).

BEAUTY PAGEANTS

Judith McConnell (MIRANDA BISHOP) represented Pennsylvania in the Miss America Pageant.

Sandra Ferguson (AMANDA CORY) also represented Pennsylvania, but in the 1985 Miss USA Pageant. Prior to that she had been second runner-up in the Miss Teen All-American Pageant.

At age seventeen, Alla Korot (JENNA NORRIS) was named Miss California T.E.E.N., a contest that emphasized academic performance and achievements.

Joseph Barbara (JOE CARLINO) was a celebrity judge at the 1996 Miss America Pageant.

Judi Evans Luciano (PAULINA CORY CARLINO) judged a Regular Guy contest sponsored by Aqua Velva aftershave.

CELEBRITY ENCOUNTERS

Lisa Peluso (LILA ROBERTS), who lives in the same neighborhood as John F. Kennedy Jr. and his wife, Carolyn Bessette Kennedy, once rode on the subway right next to the magazine publisher. She did not, however, take advantage of the opportunity to say hello to him.

Dack Rambo (GRANT HARRISON) and his twin brother Dirk were discovered in church by movie legend Loretta Young, who asked the two of them to work on her TV show.

While tending bar at the Pub Room at Arthur, which was managed by Richard Burton's wife Sybil, John Aprea (LUCAS CASTIGLIANO and ALEXANDER NIKOS) served members of such high-profile families as the Kennedys and Rockefellers.

A teenaged Patti D'Arbanville (CHRISTY CARSON) was playing chess when Andy Warhol asked her if she wanted to be in a movie. She agreed and ended up in his film *Flesh* and later in *L'amour*. D'Arbanville in turn taught

Warhol how to crochet. Warhol had also expressed an interest in John Aprea during his bartending days, but never ended up using the actor in a film.

While acting in a play directed by Sir Laurence Olivier, Stephen Schnetzer (CASS WINTHROP) could not bring himself to call the legendary actor "Larry," even though Olivier had told him to.

Richard Burgi (CHAD ROLLO) was once trapped in an elevator with movie legend Katharine Hepburn.

Julian McMahon (IAN RAIN) stuck his foot in his mouth when he met Holly Hunter at the Australian premiere of The Piano. A photographer called him over to pose for a picture with Hunter, who happened to be one of his favorite actresses. "What are you doing here?" he asked, to which she replied, "I'm in the film."

A gourmet chef, Kaitlin Hopkins (DR. KELSEY HARRISON) turned down a job offer to work as Cybill Shepherd's personal cook.

Kale Browne (MICHAEL HUDSON) once hired the late rock legend Janis Joplin to perform at a college dance. He also knew members of the Grateful Dead before they became stars.

Sharon Gabet (BRITTANY PETERSON LOVE) took off her pantyhose at a Dr. John ("Right Place Wrong Time") concert and dropped them onto the lead singer's head from her balcony seat.

While working in a Los Angeles restaurant called The Ivy, Timothy Gibbs (GARY SINCLAIR) waited on such Hollywood superstars as Sylvester Stallone and Steven Spielberg.

Among the acting students attending the same Lee Strasberg seminar as Robert Gentry (PHILIP LYONS) was screen legend Marilyn Monroe.

While out on a date, screen legend Cary Grant advised Susan Sullivan (LENORE CURTIN) to get married, have a baby, and give up her dreams of becoming an actress.

Kale Browne (MICHAEL HUDSON) once hired Janis Joplin to perform at a school dance.

© *Barry Morgenstein*

ANIMALS

Ricky Paull Goldin (DEAN FRAME) was once bitten by his pet boa constrictor.

When he was a child, Hank Cheyne (SCOTT LASALLE) rode around on a mule named Taco.

Randy Brooks (MARSHALL LINCOLN KRAMER III) owned a pet monkey.

Denise Alexander (MARY MCKINNON) runs a wildlife refuge in the mountains north of Los Angeles.

Richard Burgi (CHAD ROLLO) has rescued a number of wounded birds. While rescuing one in Central Park with Anne Heche, he remembered that he had an audition—and he had to go to it in jeans covered with bird feces.

Farm-reared James Goodwin (KEVIN ANDERSON) was driving a tractor by age eight. By the time he entered high school, he was not only a member of the Future Farmers of America, he also owned sixty sheep.

A major fan of *The Honeymooners* sitcom, Kevin McClatchy (NICK HUDSON) named his cocker spaniel Norton, after Art Carney's character on the show.

One Christmas, Laura Moss (AMANDA CORY) and her mother rescued a trio of kittens. After taking them to the vet, Moss discovered that the kittens had come from the very same cat her mother had rescued just two months previously.

MUSICAL TALENTS

Douglass Watson (MAC CORY) has sung with the New York City Opera.

Sally Spencer (M. J. McKINNON) toured as a backup singer for Perry Como, the Carpenters, Bert Convy, and John Davidson.

Randy Brooks (MARSHALL LINCOLN KRAMER III) spent five years singing with the Honolulu Symphony Orchestra.

Brandy Brown (ANGELA CORELLI) was a three-time junior vocalist champion on the nationally syndicated talent show *Star Search*.

Laurence Lau (DR. JAMIE FRAME) wrote a song called "Action," which was recorded by R&B artist Junior Walker.

Patrick Tovatt (ZANE LINDQUIST) plays the fiddle.

Brian Lane Green (SAM FOWLER) used to sing with the PTL club.

Anna Holbrook (SHARLENE FRAME) toured the country with the singing group Up With People.

Patti D'Arbanville's (CHRISTY CARSON) former boyfriend, singer Cat Stevens, wrote the song "Lady D'Arbanville" about her.

SPORTS

Having owned and shown horses since childhood, Victoria Wyndham (RACHEL CORY) has become an accomplished equestrienne. She has ridden in the United States Equestrian Team Final Selection Trials for the Olympics.

During a production of *Arsenic and Old Lace*, Mark Krassenbaum (JERRY HOCH) fell down a staircase and broke both his knees. The accident shattered his plans to one day swim in the Olympics.

David Canary (STEVE FRAME) has been the coach of his son's Little League baseball team.

Chris Bruno (DENNIS WHEELER), who once considered a career in professional baseball, has pitched for the semi-pro Long Island White Sox baseball team.

After seeing a photo layout set in the Manhattan Squash Club, Richard Burgi (CHAD ROLLO) got a job there working as a squash pro. He also competed in some tournaments.

Tina Sloan (DR. OLIVIA DELANEY) has climbed Mount Kilimanjaro and has competed in the Los Angeles and New York marathons.

Diego Serrano (TOMAS RIVERA) has played soccer for most of his life and considered turning pro when he was sixteen.

Christine Jones (JANICE FRAME) took fourteenth place in a fishing contest in the mid-1980s.

Dondre Whitfield (JESSE LAWRENCE) studied boxing with former world welterweight champion James "Buddy" McGirt.

Tom Eplin (JAKE MCKINNON) works out every day with kickboxing champion Olando Rivera. Joe Barbara (JOE CARLINO) traveled with Eplin down to Atlantic City to see Rivera win his title in 1997.

Kim Rhodes (CINDY HARRISON) has been trained in hand-to-hand, quarter-staff, rapier, and dagger combat.

Jim MacLaren (DAVID CAMPBELL) held the world record for fastest triathlon amputee, a record that he broke himself.

CRIME AND PUNISHMENT

Larry Lau (DR. JAMIE FRAME) and a group he hung around with in his younger days committed three crimes—breaking and entering, vandalism, and attempted car robbery—all in one night.

Dondre Whitfield's (JESSE LAWRENCE) father, who has served time in prison, wrote to Whitfield after seeing him in an episode of *The Cosby Show* on the rec room TV.

Chris Robinson (JASON FRAME) was arrested in the early 1980s for allegedly assaulting his estranged wife. In 1985, he was sent to prison for four months for tax evasion.

Bothered by the gang assault on a jogger in Central Park, Clayton Prince (REUBEN LAWRENCE) patrolled the New York subways as part of the Guardian Angels, the famed vigilante organization. He kept his nightly exploits a secret from his mother until just before *People* magazine intended to run a piece on him.

HOBBIES

Eric Morgan Stuart (CHRIS MADISON) avidly collects comic books, especially *The X-Men*.

The late Brent Collins (WALLINGFORD) collected Waterford crystal.

Reed Birney's (WALTER TRASK) video and laser disk collection includes more than 3,500 titles. He owns so many that he has had to search for days for a specific title someone wanted to borrow.

A true gambler at heart, Judi Evans Luciano (PAULINA CORY CARLINO) used to organize all-women poker games and once won $3,000 playing craps for six hours.

Once Rhonda Ross Kendrick (TONI BURRELL) begins or even spots a jigsaw puzzle, everything else around her takes a backseat until the puzzle is completed.

Tom Eplin (JAKE MCKINNON) pilots his own plane. During one trip to Pittsburgh, Eplin let best friend Chris Bruno (DENNIS WHEELER) take the wheel even though Bruno had never before piloted a plane.

Anne Heche (VICKY and MARLEY HUDSON) enjoys parachuting out of airplanes.

Robert Gentry (PHILIP LYONS) has built most of his own furniture.

Colleen Dion (BRETT GARDNER) competes with her sister to see who can own more cow-related memorabilia. Although her sister had a head start, Dion surpassed her, amassing more than 7,500 pieces of cow merchandise, including jeans, T-shirts, stuffed animals, and even an alarm clock. So great was her love for cows that her former husband Steve Jensen painted the walls of their bedroom white with black spots.

ODD JOBS

Charles Keating (CARL HUTCHINS), who sported one of the most identifiable hairstyles on daytime television, a silver-gray ponytail, used to work as a hairdresser.

David Forsyth (DR. JOHN HUDSON) has worked as a firefighter, paramedic, and surgical technician.

Hank Cheyne (SCOTT LASALLE) earned his law degree and renews his membership with the bar association every year.

Les Brandt (RAFAEL SANTIERO) quit his job as a marine biologist due to his fear of sharks.

Sharon Gabet (BRITTANY PETERSON) was a registered nurse.

Rhonda Lewin (VICKY HUDSON) worked as a bridal consultant.

Former hairdresser Charles Keating (CARL HUTCHINS).

© Barry Morgenstein

Jensen Buchanan (VICKY and MARLEY HUDSON) was a camp counselor in Germany.

Larry Lau (DR. JAMIE FRAME) met his agent while selling newspapers on the street in Hollywood.

Elain M. Graham (ETTA MAE BURRELL) has taught classes from the second grade all the way through the high school level.

While breaking into modeling, Mark Mortimer (NICK HUDSON) supported himself as an electrician.

Inspired by the television series *Magnum, P.I.*, Grayson McCouch (DR. MORGAN WINTHROP) worked as a licensed private investigator.

Kevin Carrigan (DEREK DANE) baked pies for New York restaurants.

Charles Grant (EVAN BATES) was a bouncer at the European disco Regine's.

Before getting into acting, Brent Collins (WALLINGFORD) was a book editor at Random House.

David Hedison (SPENCER HARRISON) has worked as a door-to-door Fuller Brush salesman and has polished silver at the Waldorf-Astoria Hotel.

Bronson Pickett (SCOTT GUTHRIE) so impressed his stockbroker with his understanding of the market that the broker offered him a job in the firm.

Kim Rhodes's (CYNTHIA HARRISON) chores as a veterinary assistant included neutering male cats, a skill she included on her résumé, which helped her land a role sight unseen.

George Reinholt (STEVE FRAME) took out ads in several newspapers, offering to escort women to parties, weddings, and Bingo. Reinholt took offense when a national tabloid published an article portraying him as a gigolo. Although Reinholt wanted to be paid for his time, sex-for-hire was not part of the deal.

Happy Birthday to Them

January

2	John Considine (VIC HASTINGS AND REGINALD LOVE)
5	Ricky Paull Goldin (DEAN FRAME)
8	Eric Scott Woods (EVAN FRAME)
13	Sharon Gabet (BRITTANY PETERSON LOVE)
19	Christine Tucci (AMANDA CORY)
21	Ann Wedgeworth (LAHOMA VANE LUCAS)
26	Allison Hossack (OLIVIA MATTHEWS)
28	Nicholas Pryor (TOM BAXTER)
30	Randy Brooks (MARSHALL LINCOLN KRAMER III)

February

1	Susan Harney (ALICE FRAME)
1	Kaitlin Hopkins (KELSEY HARRISON)
3	B. J. Jefferson (RONNIE LAWRENCE)
4	Kristen Marie (CHERYL MCKINNON)
5	Val Dufour (WALTER CURTIN)
5	Diego Serrano (TOMAS RIVERA)
12	Lisa Brenner (MAGGIE CORY)
17	Clayton Prince (REUBEN LAWRENCE)
22	Michael Rodrick (CAMERON SINCLAIR)

26   John Bolger (DR. ALTON SPADER and
     GABE MCNAMARA)

27   Sally Spencer (M. J. MCKINNON)

28   Charles Durning (GIL MCGOWAN)

March

4   John Aprea (LUCAS CASTIGLIANO and
     ALEXANDER NIKOS)

7   Mark Pinter (GRANT HARRISON)

9   Brian Lane Green (SAM FOWLER)

9   Joe Gallison (BILL MATTHEWS)

10   Ariane Munker (MARIANNE RANDOLPH)

14   Russell Todd (DR. JAMIE FRAME)

15   Chris Bruno (DENNIS WHEELER)

19   Michael M. Ryan (JOHN RANDOLPH)

21   Kathleen Widdoes (ROSE PERRINI)

23   Sandra Ferguson (AMANDA CORY)

27   Kerri Ann Darling (ALLI FOWLER)

April

1   Jordan Charney (SAM LUCAS)

7   Steve Bolster (TED CLARK)

12   Alicia Coppola (LORNA DEVON)

15   Mark Mortimer (NICK HUDSON)

17   Timothy Gibbs (GARY SINCLAIR)

18   Anna Holbrook (SHARLENE FRAME)

18   Robert Kelker-Kelly (SAM FOWLER and
     DR. SHANE ROBERTS)

Victoria Wyndham, who played both Rachel Cory and her evil lookalike, Justine Duvalier, is appropriately a Gemini.

© *Barry Morgenstein*

May

4	Matt Crane (MATT CORY)
6	Ben Masters (VIC STRANG)
7	Robin Strasser (RACHEL CORY)
10	Laurence Lau (DR. JAMIE FRAME)
12	Linda Dano (FELICIA GALLANT)
20	David Hedison (SPENCER HARRISON)
22	Ed Fry (ADAM CORY)
22	Victoria Wyndham (RACHEL CORY)
25	Anne Heche (MARLEY and VICKY HUDSON)
27	Dondre Whitfield (JESSE LAWRENCE)
30	David Ackroyd (DAVE GILCHRIST)
31	Maeve Kinkead (ANGIE PERRINI)
31	Petronia Paley (QUINN HARDING)

June

1	Morgan Freeman (ROY BINGHAM)
1	David Andrew MacDonald (JORDAN STARK)
7	Kim Rhodes (CINDY BROOKE HARRISON)
11	Stephen Schnetzer (CASS WINTHROP)
12	Nadine Stenovitch (JOSIE WATTS)
16	Kale Browne (MICHAEL HUDSON)
18	Robin Christopher (LORNA DEVON)
19	Elain R. Graham (ETTA MAE BURRELL)
23	Ted Shackelford (RAY GORDON)
29	Joy Bell (CAROLINE STAFFORD)

July

1   Henry Simmons (TYRONE MONTGOMERY)

3   Jeff Phillips (MATT CORY)

7   Amy Carlson (JOSIE WATTS)

7   Carmen Duncan (IRIS CARRINGTON WHEELER)

8   John Littlefield (GARY SINCLAIR)

12   Barbara Berjer (BRIDGET CONNELL)

12   Judi Evans Luciano (PAULINA CORY)

17   Alexandra Wilson (JOSIE WATTS)

18   Jensen Buchanan (VICKY HUDSON)

19   William Grey Espy (MITCH BLAKE)

21   Anne Meacham (LOUISE GODDARD)

22   Joanna Going (LISA GRADY)

23   Terry Davis (STACEY WINTHROP)

23   Jacqueline Brookes (BEATRICE GORDON)

24   James Goodwin (KEVIN ANDERSON)

27   Julian McMahon (IAN RAIN)

29   Robert Lupone (NEAL CORY)

29   Lisa Peluso (LILA ROBERTS CORY)

30   Richard Burgi (CHAD ROLLO)

August

4   Laurie Heineman (SHARLENE FRAME)

9   Beverlee McKinsey (IRIS CARRINGTON WHEELER)

12   Taylor Stanley (REMY WOODS)

13   Hank Cheyne (SCOTT LASALLE)

14   Rhonda Ross Kendrick (TONI BURRELL)

19   Kyra Sedgwick (JULIA SHEARER)

22   George Reinholt (STEVE FRAME)

24   Jennifer Lien (HANNAH MOORE)

25   David Canary (STEVE FRAME)

28   Russell Curry (CARTER TODD)

29   Toni Kalem (ANGIE PERRINI)

September

1   Kevin McClatchy (NICK HUDSON)

6   Judith McConnell (MIRANDA BISHOP)

7   Les Brandt (RAFAEL SANTIERO)

12   Irene Dailey (LIZ MATTHEWS)

17   Tresa Hughes (EMMA ORDWAY)

18   David Forsyth (DR. JOHN HUDSON)

24   Jacqueline Courtney (ALICE MATTHEWS FRAME)

24   Paul Michael Valley (RYAN HARRISON)

27   David Bailey (RUSS MATTHEWS)

28   Jennifer Leak (OLIVE GORDON)

29   Robert Gentry (PHILIP LYONS)

30   Susan Keith (CECILE DE POULIGNAC)

October

1   Christine Andreas (DR. TAYLOR BENSON)

9   Ellen Wheeler (VICKY and MARLEY HUDSON)

11   Gail Brown (CLARICE EWING)

17   Hilary Edson (STACEY WINTHROP)

18   Joe Morton (ABEL and LEO MARSH)

20   William Russ (BURT McGOWAN)

22   Charles Keating (CARL HUTCHINS)

25   Tom Eplin (JAKE MCKINNON)

29   Grayson McCouch (MORGAN WINTHROP)

November

1   Alla Korot (JENNA NORRIS)

1   Laura Moss (AMANDA CORY)

1   Anna Stuart (DONNA LOVE)

5   Chris Robinson (JASON FRAME)

11   Denise Alexander (MARY MCKINNON)

18   Susan Sullivan (LENORE CURTIN)

21   Dahlia Salem (SOFIA CARLINO)

27   Robert Doran (JAMIE FRAME)

27   Cathy Greene (SALLY FRAME)

29   Charles Grant (EVAN FRAME)

30   Kevin Conroy (JERRY GROVE)

December

1   Patrick Tovatt (ZANE LINDQUIST)

3   Nicolas Coster (ROBERT DELANEY)

4   Danny Markel (SAM FOWLER)

5   Joe Barbara (JOE CARLINO)

5   Lewis Arlt (DAVID THATCHER and KEN JORDAN)

6   Leon Russom (WILLIS FRAME)

11   Patrick Tovatt (ZANE LINDQUIST)

18   Ray Liotta (JOEY PERRINI)

19   Alice Barrett (FRANKIE FRAME)

28   Colleen Dion (BRETT GARDNER)

Anna Stuart (DONNA LOVE), seen here receiving
an unusual gift from Matt Crane (MATT CORY),
shares her birthday with two former castmates.

© *Barry Morgenstein*

From Hollywood to Bay City

1. What Clint Eastwood film did Beverlee McKinsey appear in while still starring on *Another World*?
   (a) *Any Which Way You Can*   (b) *Bronco Billy*
   (c) *Coogan's Bluff*   (d) *Dirty Harry*

2. Which current *Another World* actress played John Travolta's little sister in *Saturday Night Fever*?
   (a) Lisa Peluso (LILA ROBERTS CORY)
   (b) Kim Rhodes (CINDY HARRISON)
   (c) Nadine Stenovitch (JOSIE WATTS SINCLAIR)
   (d) Judi Evans Luciano (PAULINA CORY CARLINO)

3. Which of the following films from the late 1950s starred Constance Ford (ADA DAVIS)?
   (a) *Summer Love*   (b) *A Summer Place*
   (c) *Suddenly Last Summer* (d) *The Long Hot Summer*

4. In which of the following science fiction/horror films did David Hedison (SPENCER HARRISON) play the title character?
   (a) *The Fly*
   (b) *The Invisible Man*
   (c) *I Married an Alien*
   (d) *The Man with the X-Ray Eyes*

5. John Aprea (LUCAS CASTIGLIANO and ALEXANDER NIKOS) lost the role of Michael Corleone to Al Pacino but ended up playing young Tessio in which *Godfather* installment?
   (a) the original   (b) *The Godfather, Part II*
   (c) a and b   (d) *The Godfather, Part III*

6. Darlene Love originated the role of Judy Burrell, Felicia Gallant's AA sponsor, after working in what popular series of action films?

(a) Clint Eastwood's Dirty Harry films

(b) Bruce Willis's *Die Hard* series

(c) the Mel Gibson–Danny Glover *Lethal Weapon* buddy films

(d) Sylvester Stallone's *Rambo* movies

7. What horror movie monster sliced Russell Todd's (DR. JAMIE FRAME) throat while he hung upside down from a tree?

(a) Freddy Krueger in *A Nightmare on Elm Street*

(b) Jason Voorhies in *Friday the 13th, Part II*

(c) Pinhead in *Hellraiser III*

(d) Michael Myers in *Halloween IV*

8. What actor not only had a role in the Robert Altman film *A Wedding* but also worked on the script?

(a) Lewis Arlt (DAVID THATCHER and KEN JORDAN)

(b) John Aprea (LUCAS CASTIGLIANO and ALEXANDER NIKOS)

(c) John Considine (VIC HASTINGS and REGINALD LOVE)

(d) Gary Carpenter (MIKE BAUER and RAY GORDON)

9. Who played Shelley Long's husband in the Tom Cruise comedy *Losin' It*?

(a) Kale Browne (MICHAEL HUDSON)

(b) David Forsyth (DR. JOHN HUDSON)

(c) Stephen Schnetzer (CASS WINTHROP)

(d) Richard Burgi (CHAD ROLLO)

10. In between his many stints as Carl Hutchins, Charles Keating filmed a small role in what Kevin Costner movie?

(a) *Field of Dreams* (b) *The Bodyguard*

(c) *Waterworld* (d) *Dances with Wolves*

Bonus: Which of the following actresses auditioned for the role of Scarlett O'Hara in *Gone with the Wind*?

(a) Augusta Dabney (LAURA BAXTER)

(b) Vera Allen (GRANNY MATTHEWS)

(c) Audra Lindley (LIZ MATTHEWS)

(d) Constance Ford (ADA DAVIS)

Relatively Famous

VICTORIA WYNDHAM'S (RACHEL CORY) parents, Ralph and Florence Camargo, had worked on *The Guiding Light* when it aired on the radio. Decades later, after the show had moved to television, Wyndham herself landed a role on it. As a child, Wyndham's sister Felice worked on the short-lived CBS soap *Woman with a Past,* on which she played the daughter of Constance Ford (ADA DAVIS), Wyndham's future onscreen mother. Ralph Camargo worked with his daughter on *Another World*. He played the judge who married Rachel and Mac at their first wedding.

The town of Wyndham, Connecticut, was named after one of Victoria Wyndham's ancestors, a lieutenant who had sailed to America on the *Mayflower*.

Douglass Watson (MAC CORY), whose ancestors fought during the American Revolution, shares his name with that of the Indian scout who discovered Indian Springs, now the site of a Georgia state park.

Anna Stuart (DONNA LOVE) counts Pocahantas, Davy Crocket, and Dolly Madison among her ancestors.

Cowgirl Calamity Jane was born Martha Jane Canary. Among her descendants is David Canary (STEVE FRAME). David Canary's brother John is also an actor. John's brief stint on *All My Children*, where David plays twins Adam and Stuart Chandler, gave them the chance to work together.

Timothy Gibbs, who played alcoholic police officer Gary Sinclair, got to work on the show with his brother Dave, who recurred as police officer Brian Tibbs.

The late Dack Rambo (GRANT HARRISON) and his twin brother, Dirk, became childhood stars while appearing together on *The Loretta Young Show*.

Eric Roberts, brother of film superstar Julia Roberts, originated the role of Ted Bancroft.

Christine Tucci's (AMANDA CORY) brother Stanley Tucci has made a name for himself as both a screen (*The Pelican Brief*) and television (*Murder One*) star. Christine had a small role in his 1996 film *Big Night*.

Robert Lupone's (NEAL CORY) sister Patti Lupone has gained acclaim for her work on Broadway starring in *Evita, Les Miserables,* and other productions. From 1989 to 1994, she broadened her audience playing the mother in the ABC family drama *Life Goes On*.

Cali Timmins's (PAULINA CORY) siblings comprise the country-rock band The Cowboy Junkies. Timmins appeared in their video "Sun Come Up; It's Tuesday Morning."

Film actress Karen Black's (*Airport '75, Nashville*) sister Gail Brown played Rachel Cory's stepsister Clarice Hobson.

Irene Dailey's (LIZ MATTHEWS) brother Dan made some fifty films during the 1940s and '50s, including a number of musicals such as *There's No Business Like Show Business* (with Ethel Merman and Marilyn Monroe) and *Meet Me at the Fair*. He also played legendary pitcher Dizzy Dean in the baseball flick *The Pride of St. Louis*.

John Considine (VIC HASTINGS and REGINALD LOVE) grew up in a show business family. His father, John W. Considine Jr., had produced such films as *Boys Town* and *Broadway Melodies of 1936* as well as the Rudolph Valentino silent film classic *The Son of the Sheik*. John Considine's brother Tim was one of the stars of the popular 1960s Fred MacMurray sitcom *My Three Sons*, a series for which John Considine wrote scripts.

Kaitlin Hopkins's (DR. KELSEY HARRISON) mother is award-winning actress Shirley Knight, who played Helen Hunt's mother in the 1998 Jack Nicholson blockbuster *As Good As It Gets*. Hopkins had a bit part in the film. Hopkins's godmother is Kathleen Widdoes, who played Rose Perrini.

Beverlee McKinsey's (IRIS CARRINGTON) son Scott is a soap opera director. He has worked on *The Guiding Light*, where Beverlee reigned for many years as Alexandra Spaulding. He has since moved on to *General Hospital*, where his mother put in a short but memorable performance as a former mob mistress named Myrna Slaughter.

John Bolger's (DR. ALTON SPADER and GABE MCNAMARA) great uncle is Ray Bolger, best remembered as the Scarecrow in *The Wizard of Oz*.

John Bolger (DR. ALTON SPADER and GABE MCNAMARA), pictured here with Joe Barbara (JOE CARLINO), met his great uncle, Ray Bolger, once.

© *Barry Morgenstein*

In the early 1970s, Julian McMahon's (IAN RAIN) father, Sir John McMahon, served as Prime Minister of Australia.

Maeve Kinkead (ANGIE PERRINI) is married to Harry Streep, brother to Oscar-winning film actress Meryl Streep (*Sophie's Choice*, *Out of Africa*).

Rhonda Ross Kendrick (TONI BURRELL) is the daughter of singer Diana Ross and Motown founder Berry Gordy.

A number of actors have gotten their family members on the show as day players. Linda Dano's mother attended Felicia's wedding to Zane. David Forsyth's aunt played a nurse in several scenes. Judith Barcroft's father, a minister, presided over Lenore's marriage to Walter Curtin. Stephen Schnetzer's son and Alice Barrett's daughter trick-or-treated at the Cory mansion. During a flashback scene, young Jake McKinnon was played by Tom Eplin's nephew, Jamie Hager, while young Vicky Hudson was played by Ellen Wheeler's sister Danielle.

The Artists Formerly Known As . . .

VICTORIA WYNDHAM (RACHEL CORY) née Camargo began her acting career after her sister Felice had already made a name for herself on Broadway. Casting directors got somewhat confused with two dark-haired Camargo sisters auditioning for roles. In order to cease the confusion, their parents decided that Victoria should find a new last name, as Felice already had professional credits under her own name. Annoyed, Victoria picked Wyndham from her family's history. Her son, Christian, who is making a name for himself on Broadway, goes professionally by the last name Camargo.

John Beal, who originated the role of Jim Matthews, was born James Alexander Bliedung. Shepperd Strudwick, who took over the role in the mid-1960s, was born John Shepperd. Hugh Marlowe, who played Jim the longest, was born Hugh Hipple.

It was probably not surprising to Robert Kelker-Kelly (SAM FOWLER and DR. SHANE ROBERTS) that there was already a Bobby Kelly in the actors union when he decided to become an actor. He solved the problem by adding in his mother's family name, Kelker. Kelker-Kelly had wanted to distance himself somewhat emotionally from his father's last name, because his father had walked out on the family when Kelker-Kelly was a boy.

When Ricky Paull Goldin (DEAN FRAME) was starting out in the business as a child actor, his manager convinced him to drop his last name because it sounded too ethnic. He also changed the spelling of his middle name, Paul (which he then used as a last name) to Paull partly as a way to distance himself from his father, Paul Goldin, who had left Ricky and his mother years earlier.

Because the actors union already had an Eric Stuart among its ranks, Eric Morgan Stuart (CHRIS MADISON) decided to add in a middle name. He had already been thinking of doing so just for effect. Rather than go with his given middle name, he opted to use his stepfather's name, Morgan.

Gail Brown (CLARICE EWING) and her sister, film star Karen Black, were born with the last name Ziegler. They each chose more colorful stage names, Karen opting for Black and Gail for Brown.

Hank Cheyne (SCOTT LASALLE) had to change his name because there was already a Henry Garcia in the Screen Actors Guild. He considered using his father's first name, Fidel, but ultimately shortened Cheyenne, the city where his mother was born, into Cheyne.

During the 1980s, with performers like Madonna and Prince becoming international superstars, Jackee Harry (LILY MASON) decided to drop her last name and was billed simply as Jackee. In the 1990s, she resumed using her surname.

Although Charles Grant had worked on *The Edge of Night* as Charles Flohe, by the time he took on the role of Evan Bates, he had changed his last name to the more easily pronounced Grant. Ironically, Grant's character, born Earl Frame, had changed his own name before arriving in Bay City.

Both Dack Rambo (GRANT HARRISON) and his twin brother, Dirk Rambo, changed their names when they went into show business. They had been born Norman and Orman Rambo respectively.

Rambo's onscreen father, David Hedison (SPENCER HARRISON), started off life as Ara Heditsian. His father Anglicized his name, making him Albert Hedison. After he signed a contract with Fox, the studio executives encouraged Hedison to find a first name more befitting a leading man than Al. Hedison chose his middle name, David.

A number of actors on the show have used their middle names as either their first or last names, such as Douglass Watson (MAC CORY), born Larkin Douglass Watson, and Russell Todd (JAMIE FRAME), born Russell Todd Goldberg.

By the time Gary Pillar (MIKE BAUER) returned to *Another World* in the 1970s to play Ray Gordon, the actor was known as Gary Carpenter.

Although George Bush's wife, Barbara, was one of the most famous women in the country in the mid-1980s, married as she was to the vice president of the United States, she was not in the acting union. Therefore, actress Barbara Bush, who played Dawn Rollo, was free to keep her own name. In recent years however, Barbara Bush, the actress, has changed her last name to Tyson.

When Lewis Arlt (DAVID THATCHER and KEN JORDAN) started writing scripts for soap operas, he used the pseudonym William Burritt (his two middle names) to keep his actor friends from learning that he was writing their dialogue.

Many actresses, like Judi Evans Luciano (PAULINA CORY CARLINO), opt to add their husband's last name to their own. When Sandi Ferguson (AMANDA CORY) got married, she took her husband's last name, Reinhardt. She also modified Sandi into the more mature sounding Sandra. After the marriage broke up, she reclaimed her maiden name but kept Sandra.

Earlier in his career, Jack Betts (LOUIS ST. GEORGE) used the name Hunt Powers, a masculine sounding name in the style of movie stars of the day like Rock Hudson, Troy Donahue, and Tab Hunter.

Taylor Stanley's (REMY WOODS) family and longtime friends call her by her given first name, Michelle. She was nicknamed Taylor after a soap opera character.

Ariana Chase, who took over the role of Marianne Randolph, later rechristened herself to symbolize the sense of rebirth she was feeling. During the 1970s, Chase had worked on a number of soap operas under the name Ariane Munker, which itself started out as Muenker.

Sandra Ferguson
(AMANDA CORY)
has changed her
name to Reinhardt
and back again.
© Barry Morgenstein

While Steve Fletcher (HANK KENT) was working on *One Life to Live*, he made an odd bet with the brother of his then-girlfriend, soap actress Nana Visitor (later a star of *Star Trek: Deep Space Nine*). If Fletcher could not bellyslide through the snow as far as he claimed he could, he would have to change his name. After Fletcher lost the bet, Visitor suggested the new last name Blizzard because of the snow that had instigated the bet. Fletcher changed his name legally and professionally to Blizzard. Once he and Visitor broke up, he saw no reason to keep his frosty moniker.

Sometimes small, almost unnoticeable changes can make a significant difference in a career. For years, Elain M. Graham (ETTA MAE BURRELL) had been spelling her first name with an extra e: *Elaine*. It wasn't until she took a close look at her birth certificate that she realized her name was officially spelled *Elain*. A numerologist advised her to go back to spelling her name as it was originally given to her. As soon as she did, things started to turn around for the better in various parts of Graham's life, including her career.

Long Night's Journey into Day

1. On what popular long-running Western series did David Canary (STEVE FRAME) play a ranch hand named Candy?

(a) *Gunsmoke*   (b) *Bonanza*   (c) *Wagon Train*   (d) *Have Gun Will Travel*

2. Which future *Another World* actor played Will Adams in the Michael Landon–created frontier drama *Father Murphy*?

(a) Robert Kelker-Kelly (SAM FOWLER)

(b) Brian Lane Green (SAM FOWLER)

(c) Timothy Gibbs (GARY SINCLAIR)

(d) John Littlefield (GARY SINCLAIR)

3. On what Irwin Allen–produced science fiction series of the 1960s did David Hedison (SPENCER HARRISON) star as Captain Lee Crane?

(a) *Time Tunnel*   (b) *Land of the Giants*

(c) *Lost in Space*   (d) *Voyage to the Bottom of the Sea*

4. On what popular primetime soap did Dack Rambo (GRANT HARRISON) play a long-lost cousin named Jack?

(a) *Dallas*   (b) *Dynasty*   (c) *Paper Dolls*   (d) *Falcon Crest*

5. On which primetime soap opera did John Aprea (LUCAS CASTIGLIANO and ALEXANDER NIKOS) play a mobster named Manny Vasquez?

(a) *Dynasty*   (b) *Dynasty II: The Colbys*

(c) *Knots Landing*   (d) *Falcon Crest*

6. Which cast member played Patty Duke's son on *Hail to the Chief* and dated Jane Curtin's daughter on *Kate and Allie*?

(a) Matt Crane (MATT CORY)

(b) Hank Cheyne (SCOTT LASALLE)

(c) Brian Lane Green (SAM FOWLER)

(d) Ricky Paull Goldin (DEAN FRAME)

7. On what 1980s crime drama did Patti D'Arbanville (CHRISTY CARSON) and Gerald Anthony (RICK MADISON) have recurring roles as a record company executive and a priest, respectively?

(a) *Crime Story*   (b) *Miami Vice*   (c) *21 Jump Street*   (d) *Wiseguy*

8. Christopher Norris, who played Jordan Stark's assistant, Ms. Allen, played Nurse Gloria "Ripples" Brancusi on what 1980s medical drama?

(a) *Medical Center*   (b) *St. Elsewhere*

(c) *Nightingales*   (d) *Trapper John, M.D.*

9. On the daytime drama *Return to Peyton Place*, Joe Gallison (BILL MATTHEWS) took on the role of Steven Cord, a role played on the primetime series by which future *Another World* actor?

(a) Hugh Marlowe (JIM MATTHEWS)

(b) Doug Watson (MAC CORY)

(c) James Douglas (ELIOT CARRINGTON)

(d) George Reinholt (STEVE FRAME)

10. Which member of *The Brady Bunch* played Leigh Hobson on *Another World* in 1981?

(a) Maureen McCormick (MARCIA)   (b) Barry Williams (GREG)

(c) Eve Plumb (JAN)   (d) Christopher Knight (PETER)

Bonus: Which one of the bunch did Jennifer Runyon (SALLY FRAME) play in the 1988 TV movie *A Very Brady Christmas*?

(a) Marcia

(b) Jan

(c) Cindy

(d) Carol, the mother, in a flashback sequence

Unscripted Kisses

ELLEN WHEELER (VICKY and MARLEY LOVE) and Tom Eplin (JAKE MCKINNON) did not start dating until after they had already been rooming together with her brother. Eplin had fallen into a public and bicoastal romance with Tracey Bregman from *The Young and the Restless*. The relationship, Eplin has admitted, was based strongly on physical attraction, and, at one point, it looked as though he would be asking Bregman to marry him. The relationship with Bregman hit a snag when the press began reporting rumors of a relationship between Eplin and Wheeler. Wheeler's own feelings of jealousy over Bregman forced her to realize that she liked Eplin as more than a friend and roommate. Wheeler and Eplin eloped to Las Vegas and were married by a Mormon bishop in the same hotel suite where Elvis Presley had once shot up a TV set. Were that not ominous enough, Wheeler wore the very same engagement ring and wedding band that Eplin had picked out for a previous fiancée. The marriage lasted a little over two years.

Tom Eplin also dated Lisa Peluso (LILA ROBERTS) for two months in the early 1990s, and was married to former Miss America Courtney Gibbs, who did a short stint on *All My Children* as an assistant district attorney.

In addition to Eplin, Peluso dated a band member from ZZ Top ("Legs," "Sharp Dressed Man") and Perry Stephens, whose ex-wife she would later play on *Loving*.

Rick Porter (LARRY EWING) proposed to Deborah Hobart (AMY DUDLEY) on New Year's Eve in front of a fireplace. They had, along with several other soap opera actors, rented a house in the mountains for the holiday. While the others prepared for a party at a nearby lodge, Porter asked Hobart if they could stay behind and spend some private time together. As the clock struck twelve, Porter rang in the New Year by asking Hobart to marry him.

William Prince and Augusta Dabney married while playing Ken and Laura Baxter. They had met while playing husband and wife on the NBC soap opera *Young Doctor Malone*. They went on to play husband and wife on a number of other soaps.

Although Hank Cheyne (SCOTT LASALLE) and Missy Hughes (SARA MONTAIGNE) joined the show around the same time, they never got to work together before Sara was written off the show. Her onscreen kisses were reserved for Richard Burgi as Chad Rollo. Real life proved to be a different story. Cheyne not only got to know Hughes, the two eventually married.

In 1997, Anne Heche became half of the most famous lesbian couple in America when her lover, comic actress Ellen DeGeneres, came out of the closet. In an interview on *Oprah*, Heche revealed that she had never been with another woman or considered it until she met DeGeneres. Prior to meeting DeGeneres, Heche had been involved romantically with two of her male co-stars: Richard Burgi, who played Chad Rollo on *Another World*, and actor-comedian Steve Martin, with whom she worked on the film *A Simple Twist of Fate*.

Burgi, who thought Heche was a bimbo when he first met her, had also casually dated castmate Sally Spencer, whose M. J. McKinnon had been one of the hookers Chad used to pimp.

Robert Kelker-Kelly (SAM FOWLER and DR. SHANE ROBERTS) met his first wife, Linda, a production assistant on the show, in part thanks to a TV production workers' strike. Kelker-Kelly had invited everyone from *Another World* to an afternoon party at his apartment, but because of the strike only three people showed up. One of them was Linda, whom he then invited out to lunch. Hours later, the two returned and watched the sunset from his fire escape. Despite its romantic beginnings, the subsequent marriage did not last very long.

Kelker-Kelly is currently married to Miriam Parrish, an actress whom he met while working on *Days of Our Lives*. Kelker-Kelly, who grew close to Parrish while helping her with her homework, initially fought his attraction to her because of their age difference: he was in his early thirties, and she was in her late teens. As soon as she turned eighteen, they moved full speed ahead with their romance. Kelker-Kelly proposed to Parrish onstage in front of an audience after she came to see him in a play.

Executive producer Christopher Goutman is married to Marcia McCabe, who played hit person Bunny Eberhardt. The two met while acting together on the now defunct *Search for Tomorrow*.

Patricia Estrin and Rod Arrants met while playing brother and sister on the *Another World* quasi-spin-off *Lovers and Friends*. While that show was taken off the air for retooling, Arrants's character, Austin Cushing, was moved temporarily to Bay City while Estrin created a whole new character, Joan Barnard. The two later married and subsequently divorced.

By the time Robin Christopher took over the role of Lorna Devon, Lorna's relationship with Matt Cory (Matt Crane) was a thing of the past. Even though they didn't play lovers onscreen, a relationship sparked between Christopher and Crane. In 1998, the pair announced their plans to marry. Prior to Christopher, Crane had briefly dated another "Robin," Robyn Griggs (MAGGIE CORY) but the two decided that they would do better keeping their relationship at the friendship level.

Kaitlin Hopkins (KELSEY HARRISON) met film actor Judge Reinhold (*Beverly Hills Cop*) when she was performing at the Cinegrill nightclub in Hollywood. Reinhold was so taken with her that he asked her out that very evening. Shy, Hopkins turned him down, but Reinhold would not give up easily. He sent her a single gardenia every day for a week, then asked her out again, this time to the premiere of his movie *Daddy's Dying . . . Who's Got the Will?* The couple went together so long that they started referring to each other as husband and wife, though they never officially married.

After Chris Bruno landed the role of Dennis Wheeler, his friends kidded him about working with all those beautiful actresses. Bruno dismissed their jokes, planning to concentrate on doing the best acting job he could. Ironically, within one month on the show, he started dating Alicia Coppola (LORNA DEVON). Coppola had liked him from the very first day she saw him standing by the wardrobe department. She had no idea who he was or that he was an actor on the show; she just knew that she intended to get to know him better. The two worked hard to keep their backstage romance a secret. They did not go public until the show's Christmas party in 1991. After breaking up with Coppola, Bruno moved on to pop singer Deborah Gibson ("Only in My Dreams," "Electric Youth").

Linda Dano (FELICIA GALLANT) met her husband, Frank Attardi, an art director for an advertising company, when he hired her for a commercial. They dated for several years before eventually tying the knot. Attardi has turned up on *Another World* several times, including appearing as an extra at Felicia's three weddings. Attardi recurred for a brief time as Beau Wexler, an agent and would-be suitor whose romantic overture Felicia turned down.

Like Linda Dano, Judi Evans Luciano (PAULINA CORY CARLINO) has gotten to work with her husband, CNBC camera operator Mike Luciano. In 1996, Mike played a customer at Carlino's, the restaurant run by Paulina and her husband Joe.

Susan Keith, who originated the role of Cecile de Poulignac in 1979, is married in real life to James Kiberd, who currently plays Trevor Dillon on *All My Children* and had a short-term role on *Another World* as Dustin Trent in 1989. The two met while playing lovers on the ABC soap *Loving*. Had it been up to Kiberd, they never would have worked together at all. After Keith's audition, Kiberd told the producers not to hire her, claiming she seemed too cold for the part.

Prior to Kiberd, Keith dated her former castmate Ray Liotta (JOEY PERRINI). In addition to Keith, Liotta also dated Vicky Dawson, who played his wife, Eileen Simpson Perrini.

Nancy Frangione, who took over the role of Cecile from Keith, had a backstage romance of her own. While Cecile pursued Sandy Cory (Chris Rich) for his money, Frangione went after Rich for love alone—which is probably why the Cecile-Sandy merger lasted just a year and the Frangione-Rich marriage more than a decade.

Stephen Schnetzer (CASS WINTHROP) met his wife Nancy Snyder while the two were working together on the ABC soap *One Life to Live*. Schnetzer played Marcello Salsa, a blue-collar worker and personal trainer; Snyder played Katrina Karr, his love interest, an ex-prostitute. Schnetzer was the first actor with whom Snyder shared a stage kiss. When she asked Schnetzer for advice on how to do it, he told her that they should simply kiss. The two worked together more recently during the *Another World* storyline in which Cass suffered from manic depression. Snyder came on for a short-term stint as Cass's psychiatrist, Dr. Emily Bradford.

Carla Borelli, who played fashion designer Barbara Van Arkdale, is married to former *Edge of Night* leading man Donald May. The two met while working together on the *Another World* spin-off *Texas*.

Ricky Paull Goldin (DEAN FRAME) has dated his share of soap opera actresses. Upon meeting Alexandra Wilson, who played Josie Watts, he was instantly smitten with her, and she with him. They tested the dating waters but decided against pursuing it further. He considers Melissa Reeves (JENNIFER HORTON, *Days of Our Lives*) his first true love. After losing her, he dated her costar on that soap, Charlotte Ross (EVE DONOVAN), whom he broke up with right after the Daytime Emmy Awards. Of his romantic relationships, his engagement to *Baywatch* babe Yasmine Bleeth, who also worked on *Ryan's Hope* and *One Life to Live,* probably received the most media coverage. Ironically Goldin met Bleeth while working in a play in which her character dumped his.

When Christine Tucci (AMANDA CORY) first met Paul Michael Valley (RYAN HARRISON), she thought he was gay. That mistaken first impression was discarded fairly quickly, and the two were dating by the end of Tucci's first

Paul Michael Valley (Ryan Harrison) and Christine Tucci
(Amanda Cory) found love on the set.
© Barry Morgenstein

month on the show. They eventually moved in together and set a wedding date, but broke up before they ever made it to the altar. Before Tucci, Paul Michael Valley was engaged to Staige Prince, an actress from *Loving*. He also briefly dated Cady McClain (Dixie Cooney, *All My Children*), whom he had met at the *Soap Opera Digest* Awards.

Although Caitlin Ewing's romance with Sally Frame ended tragically with Sally's death, Thomas Ian Griffith and Mary Page Keller (Caitlin Ewing and Sally Frame) sparked as a couple both onscreen and off. The two were married in 1991, several years after they had left the show. The following year, they made their first film together, the action flick *Ulterior Motives*, which Griffith also wrote.

Beverlee McKinsey (Iris Cory Carrington) worked with her late husband, Berkeley Harris, on the now defunct CBS soap opera *Love Is a Many Splendored Thing*.

John Tillinger's marriage to Dorothy Lyman (Gwen Parrish) was coming to an end when he took over the role of Cory family servant Leonard Brooks. Despite their marital problems, the two managed to work together on the show for two years.

After knowing one another literally for decades, Denise Alexander (Mary McKinnon) and her longtime love Richard Colla, with whom she worked on *Days of Our Lives*, finally tied the knot. The two also worked together on the 1978 Katharine Hepburn film *Olly, Olly, Oxen Free*—Colla directed, Alexander worked as still photographer and production coordinator.

Anna Stuart (Donna Love) met her longtime love, Jesse Doran, when she helped him find his dog, which had gotten lost in Central Park. An actor, Doran had a short stint as mob boss Marius Sloan on *Another World*. He was more recently seen in the 1998 kids' action film *Small Soldiers*.

Cali Timmins (Paulina Cory) fell in love with Geoffrey Pierson, with whom she worked on the ABC soap opera *Ryan's Hope*. On that show, Timmins's character Maggie harbored an unrequited attraction for her brother-in-law Frank Ryan, played by Pierson. Pierson turned up on *Another World* as a record company tycoon in 1992, but by that time Timmins had already left the role of Paulina.

Sharon Gabet (Brittany Peterson Love), who once referred to Bob Woods (Bo Buchanan, *One Life to Live*) as "the man that got away," married Larry Joshua, who worked on *Search for Tomorrow* in the early 1980s. For their wedding, Gabet wore the very same dress her character, Raven, got married in on *Edge of Night*.

Kale Browne (Michael Hudson) was married for several years to Karen Allen, perhaps best remembered as Indiana Jones's love interest in *Raiders of the Lost Ark*. Browne and Allen got to work together several years ago on the Jeanne Tripplehorn–Dylan McDermott romantic comedy *'Til There Was You*.

Mark Pinter (Grant Harrison) and Colleen Zenk Pinter (Barbara Ryan, *As the World Turns*) have evolved into one of the more respected real-life couples in daytime. When their relationship began, though, it caused more than a little scandal. They met when Pinter played Brian McColl, one of Barbara's boyfriends on *ATWT,* in the mid-1980s. At that time, they were both married and had children with other people. Pinter suspects that his relationship with Zenk led to his termination from the show. The couple has been married for several years now and has a child of their own. Prior to landing the role of Grant Harrison, Pinter had been staying home raising the baby while his wife worked.

John Littlefield took over the role of Gary Sinclair just as Gary's plotline began to intersect with Cindy Harrison (Kim Rhodes). Although new to the show, Littlefield and Rhodes were not strangers to one another. They dated back when they went to college together. Littlefield, who has described Rhodes as "a great girlfriend," has taken full blame for the failure of their relationship.

Real-Life Wedding Album

CHARLES KEATING (CARL HUTCHINS) risked court-martial to marry his wife, Mary. The same weekend that he planned to tie the knot, he was confined to his barracks for not making his bunk up properly. Instead of putting his wedding on hold, he went AWOL. He escaped disciplinary action thanks to a superior officer who took a liking to him and had him transferred to the army's entertainment division.

Anna Holbrook (SHARLENE FRAME HUDSON) met her husband, Bruce Holbrook, when she was fifteen years old. He took her to his sister's cotillion, where he stepped on her toes and sweated profusely over her dress. By the end of the night, Anna was ready to throw in the towel and end the relationship before it had even begun. Bruce, however, had fallen in love. Anna agreed to go out with him again, and the two dated on and off through high school and college. When it came time to pop the question, Bruce arranged with Anna's parents for them to leave the patio door leading to her bedroom unlocked. He snuck into her room during the middle of the night, sat on the edge of her bed, and asked her to marry him. She said yes, and they have been together since 1979.

At a high school reunion, Jensen Buchanan (VICKY and MARLEY LOVE) ran into Gray O'Brien, an old boyfriend who had dumped her for another girl. When he asked her to dance, she turned him down. During the course of the evening, her resentment melted away. They not only danced, they reminisced about the old days. O'Brien had obviously learned from his teenage mistake and was not about to let Buchanan get away a second time. Four months after that reunion, he asked her to marry him and she accepted.

John Considine (REGINALD LOVE) and his wife, Astrid, planned their wedding like a surprise party. Friends and family had shown up at Considine's house on December 24, 1984, expecting a simple Christmas Eve gathering. At one point, John announced that he had asked Astrid to marry him and she had accepted. After making a joke about hating long engagements, he dropped the real surprise: They were getting married right then and there.

Marcus Smythe (PETER LOVE) normally ran every morning at seven o'clock. One day, he had a difficult time dragging himself out of bed. When he finally got to the park, he found himself running behind a beautiful woman, to whom the normally shy Smythe forced himself to say hello. Although he believes that fate brought them together, the limousine service they hired for the wedding nearly kept them apart. The limo hired to bring Smythe to the church forgot to pick him up and Smythe had to hail a cab. After the ceremony, the limo that was to transport the newlyweds to the reception wouldn't start. Because all the guests had already left the parking lot, Mr. and Mrs. Smythe spent their first ninety minutes as husband and wife waiting for a jumpstart.

Laurie Landry (NICOLE LOVE) married Carl Mueller on August 19, 1987. The date was special to Landry, as it was her parents' fortieth wedding anniversary. Her parents themselves had gotten married on her grandparents' fortieth wedding anniversary.

Hilary Edson (STACEY WINTHROP) married stockbroker Lyon Polk on the Virgin Island of St. Barth's, where Polk had proposed to her several months before. While sailing, Edson dove off the side of the boat for a swim. The bracelet that Polk had given her as a wedding present slid off her wrist and into the water. An hour later, Edson's guests (forty friends and family members had traveled to the island with them) rescued a woman who had been chased by a manta ray while snorkeling with her husband. Once the woman's husband confirmed that his wife was fine, he headed back into the water. Although she considered it a million-to-one shot, Edson asked the snorkeler to keep an eye out for her bracelet. Half an hour later, the man resurfaced holding the bracelet Edson had lost.

James Goodwin (KEVIN ANDERSON) asked his wife to marry him on Christmas Day 1982. Instead of simply giving her the ring, he concocted a treasure hunt that led her to a bowl of nuts. She opened each nut until she found the one with the ring hidden inside.

While Judi Evans and CNBC cameraman Mike Luciano were vacationing in the Virgin Islands, Luciano arranged for them to take a private sunset cruise. As they were sailing around, Luciano pretended to reach into his bag for nose spray but instead pulled out an engagement ring and popped the question. After she accepted, Luciano asked, "I know you live in a world of romance. Did I do okay?" Evans replied that it was a better proposal than she had played out on any of her soaps. The couple later married at Evans's home in New Jersey. Jensen Buchanan (VICKY and MARLEY HUDSON) was the matron of honor. During the reception, Luciano toasted his new bride with a bottle of beer from the same case they had bought on their first date. It was a beautiful end to a day that had started out horribly. Like many brides-to-be, Judi Evans had been struggling to lose weight before her wedding. In addition to dieting, she had stayed away from alcohol. She avoided drinking completely until the night before the wedding. After months of dieting and a self-imposed prohibition, her stomach did not take well to three glasses of wine and a plate of food she was unaccustomed to eating. She spent the night before her wedding in the bathroom throwing up.

John Aprea (LUCAS CASTIGLIANO and ALEXANDER NIKOS) has been married three times, but has never had a traditional wedding ceremony. His first marriage was conducted in New York City Hall. He eloped for his subsequent weddings, once to Santa Barbara and the other time to Las Vegas.

Colleen Dion (BRETT GARDNER) met her future husband Steve Jensen while interviewing for a real estate job at his firm. Two days later, she moved in with him. Soon thereafter, they began planning their wedding, but kept running into obstacles because of their religious differences. Dion is Catholic, Jensen is Jewish. At one point, Dion suggested that they should just elope to Las Vegas. The subject was dropped and revisited over and over for a few weeks until Jensen drove her out to Los Angeles International Airport one night. The next flight to Vegas, they learned, was leaving in half an hour. Jensen gave Dion thirty minutes to make up her mind: hop on the plane and tie the knot or drop the idea of getting married altogether. After the wedding, the newlyweds discovered that all the decent hotels in Vegas were booked solid. Exhausted from their trip, they crashed for the night in a second-rate motel with mirrored ceilings. Their honeymoon trip to Mexico turned out to be a trial in and of itself as Dion ended up sick for the better part of it. The marriage, which began just five weeks after they met, lasted from 1988 to 1992.

Robert Kelker-Kelly married Linda Kattner, a production assistant on the show, shortly after his character Sam Fowler married Amanda Cory. After enacting all the hassle that went into Sam and Amanda's nuptials, Kelker-Kelly decided to keep his upcoming wedding very small. Less than a dozen people attended the lakeside ceremony.

Just one week before Eric Morgan Stuart (CHRIS MADISON) was to marry his wife Kim, her father, Alex, died. Despite the tragedy, the couple decided to go ahead with their wedding plans. As they were jetting away to their honeymoon destination, Kim Stuart pulled down the tray table in front of her only to discover the name *Alex* written upon it. She and Eric took it as a sign that her father had been with them on their wedding day.

Alumni Newsletter

CHARLES KEATING was continually surprised that the writers could never craft a worthwhile storyline for Morgan Freeman, who played architect Roy Bingham for eighteen months in the early 1980s. While the soap opera couldn't find material for Freeman, Hollywood certainly has. Since leaving *Another World*, he has made more than thirty films, including *Seven*, *Kiss the Girls* and its follow-up *Along Came a Spider*, the Clint Eastwood Western *Unforgiven*, the Civil War drama *Glory*, and the meteor film *Deep Impact*. He has picked up Oscar nominations for playing a pimp in *Street Smart,* a chauffeur in *Driving Miss Daisy*, and a prisoner in *The Shawshank Redemption*.

Eric Roberts's (TED BANCROFT) first film, *King of the Gypsies*, earned him a Golden Globe nomination for Best Film Debut. He earned subsequent Golden Globe nominations for *Star 80* and *Runaway Train*. For his work in *Runaway Train* Roberts also earned an Oscar nomination as Best Supporting Actor. In the twenty-one years since he left daytime, Roberts has made fifty feature films.

Ray Liotta (JOEY PERRINI) has become one of the more successful actors in Hollywood, starring in *GoodFellas*, *Field of Dreams*, *Unlawful Entry*, *Something Wild* (which earned him a Golden Globe nomination), and the HBO original production of *The Rat Pack*, in which he played Frank Sinatra. No one can accuse him, though, of having forgotten his daytime roots. After promoting the police drama *Copland* on *CBS This Morning*, which is taped in the same building as *As the World Turns*, Liotta went looking for his former

TV mother, Kathleen Widdoes (ROSE PERRINI), who plays Emma Snyder on *ATWT*. He once went running out of his hotel in bare feet to say hello when he saw Victoria Wyndham (RACHEL CORY) passing by.

Many young actors who leave daytime do so with the intention of trying their luck in feature films and primetime television. Ironically, Anne Heche (VICKY and MARLEY HUDSON), who has become a prominent film actress, did not leave *Another World* with any such game plan. She left the show to study at Parson's School of Design in New York. Those plans were sidelined by an offer to work in the Jessica Lange TV movie *O Pioneers*. Since then, Heche has become one of the busiest actresses in Hollywood, playing Johnny Depp's wife in *Donnie Brasco*, a geologist in the action adventure *Volcano*, the Janet Leigh role in the remake of *Psycho*, and a starring role opposite Harrison Ford in the romantic adventure *Six Days Seven Nights*. Her political thriller, *Return to Paradise*, featured former castmate Anna Holbrook (SHARLENE FRAME).

Heche also had a small but memorable role in the teen horror flick *I Know What You Did Last Summer*, penned by *Scream* writer Kevin Williamson, whom she met on *Another World*. Williamson played one of the office workers in the video production company. The two have remained friends ever since.

During the 1970s, Audra Lindley (LIZ MATTHEWS) became famous as the sexually frustrated housewife Helen Roper on the provocative sitcom *Three's Company*. When Lindley and her TV husband Norman Fell were spun off into their own sitcom, *The Ropers*, Ann Wedgeworth (LAHOMA VANE LUCAS) joined *Three's Company* for a season as yet another sexually frustrated resident in the apartment complex.

The Burt Reynolds sitcom *Evening Shade* cast Wedgeworth as yet another woman consumed with lust. Playing her husband, town physician Harlan Elldridge, was Charles Durning, who originated the role of Ada Davis's (Constance Ford) third husband, Gil McGowan. *Evening Shade* also starred

Michael Jeeter, who did day work as a jockey on *Another World*, and Elizabeth Ashley, who played Frankie's mother Emma for several months in 1990, right before *Shade* debuted.

Dolph Sweet, who took over the role of police detective Gil McGowan from Durning, stayed with the show until his character was blown up. He turned up as another police detective in the 1980s Nell Carter sitcom *Gimme a Break!*

William Russ, who played Gil's son Burt, went on to play father to Ben Savage in the ABC sitcom *Boy Meets World*.

Thomas Ian Griffith, so popular as the heroic Caitlin Ewing, played the sadistic karate teacher in the third *Karate Kid* movie and more recently king of the vampires in John Carpenter's *Vampires*. Among his more notable TV movies, he played Rock Hudson in an ABC biopic.

Griffith's wife, Mary Page Keller, who played Sally Frame, has built a career for herself outside of daytime. She worked on a number of sitcoms, including *Duet, Baby Talk,* and *Get a Life.* Currently, she plays Iris in the WB series *Zoe, Duncan, Jack & Jane.*

Both David Ackroyd (DR. DAVE GILCHRIST) and Ted Shackelford (RAY GORDON) played the role of J. R. Ewing's alcoholic brother Gary. Ackroyd originated the role in a two-part episode of *Dallas*. When the producers spoke to him about playing Gary in the spin-off, *Knots Landing*, he turned it down, opting instead to work on the primetime drama *Little Women*. The role was then offered to Shackelford, who played Gary for fourteen seasons.

In between writing romance novels and getting herself killed playing amateur detective, Julia Shearer considered a career as a movie star. She was even cast as Rachel Cory in a film about the goings-on in Bay City. Although her untimely death prevented Julia from making any more films, Kyra Sedgwick, who originated the role, has done well for herself in Hollywood. She has worked with Tom Cruise in the Oliver Stone Vietnam drama *Born on the Fourth of July,* Julia Roberts in the adulterous comedy *Something to Talk About,* and John Travolta in the tearjerker *Phenomenon.*

Replacing Kyra Sedgwick in the role of Julia Shearer was Faith Ford, who went on to play beauty pageant winner turned reporter Corky Sherwood on the long-running CBS sitcom *Murphy Brown.* Recently, she landed her own sitcom, *Maggie Winters.* Ford's costars on *Murphy Brown* included two *AW* alumni. Charles Kimbrough, who played uptight anchor Jim Dial, did day work as a doctor at Bayside General. Several seasons into *Murphy Brown,* Christopher Rich (SANDY CORY) began a recurring role as a slightly dimwitted newsman.

For one month in between Robert Kelker-Kelly and Danny Markel, Thomas Gibson played the role of Sam Fowler. Primetime TV fans now know him as one half of the titular sitcom couple *Dharma and Greg.*

Playing Gibson's mother on *Dharma and Greg* is Susan Sullivan (LENORE CURTIN). In 1997, Sullivan played Cameron Diaz's mother in the Julia Roberts comedy *My Best Friend's Wedding.* Although she is currently making a name for herself in comedy, Sullivan is best known as Maggie Gioberti from the primetime serial *Falcon Crest.*

In the early 1970s, Rue McClanahan wreaked havoc on the Randolph house as the psychopathic housekeeper Caroline Johnson. A year after leaving the show, she ended up on *Maude* as Bea Arthur's best friend Vivian. McClanahan and Arthur worked together again in the '80s on NBC's *The Golden Girls.* There McClanahan won an Emmy as the sexually active Southern belle Blanche Deveraux. Among the series McClanahan starred in between *Maude* and *The Golden Girls* was *Mama's Family,* a spin-off of *The Carol Burnett Show,* where she played an aunt by marriage to Dorothy Lyman (GWEN PARRISH).

Lyman landed *Mama's Family* mainly because of her work on *All My Children.* Carol Burnett, a fan of the soap, enjoyed Lyman's work and wanted her for the part of Naomi. After *Mama's Family,* Lyman had short stints on other soaps (*Generations* and *The Bold and the Beautiful*) as well as a recurring role on the acclaimed ABC drama *Life Goes On*, playing the mother of an HIV-positive teenager (Chad Lowe). Lyman shifted her energy behind the camera to direct the Fran Drescher sitcom *The Nanny*. For an episode in which Fran visited California, Lyman stepped back in front of the cameras to play a director on *The Young and the Restless*.

Christina Pickles (COUNTESS ELENA DE POULIGNAC) traded in her title for a bedpan when she made the move from daytime to primetime. With its continuing storylines, *St. Elsewhere* played out much like a daytime drama, and few of its characters led a more soap-operatic life than Pickles's much-married, drug-addicted Nurse Helen Rosenthal. More recently, Pickles has been recurring as Ross and Monica's overbearing mother on the sitcom *Friends*.

Richard Burgi, who played reformed pimp Chad Rollo, is now fighting crime in the UPN sci-fi police series *The Sentinel*. Burgi's character, police detective James Ellison, is something of a superhero, a former army captain whose five senses have all been heightened.

When it comes to playing superheroes, few actors can top Kevin Conroy's (JERRY GROVE) current gig. Every afternoon and Saturday morning, he provides the voice of Batman and his alter ego Bruce Wayne in not one but two shows, *Batman: The Animated Series* and *Batman Beyond*.

Like Conroy, Jennifer Lien (HANNAH MOORE) lends her voice to a Saturday morning cartoon series: the animated version of the sci-fi blockbuster *Men in Black*. Lien also played the alien Kes on the sci-fi series *Star Trek: Voyager*.

Jackee Harry is one of the very few actors to balance a daytime and primetime series simultaneously. Daytime knew her as *Another World*'s singer Lily Mason while primetime knew her as the vampish Sandra on the NBC sitcom 227. After a year of juggling both series, Jackee left daytime to concentrate on 227, where she stayed till its cancellation in 1990. She made her film debut two years later in the Rodney Dangerfield comedy *Ladybugs,* and currently stars in the WB sitcom *Sister, Sister*.

Future movie actress Anne Heche (Vicky and Marley Hudson)
with former boyfriend, *Sentinel* star Richard Burgi (Chad Rollo).

© Robin Platzer, Images

Jodi Lyn O'Keefe, who played the troublemaking teen Maggie Cory, has made two recent teen films: the horror flick *Halloween H2O: Twenty Years Later* and the romantic comedy *She's All That*.

Diego Serrano (TOMAS RIVERA) was one of the first actors cast in the *Party of Five* spin-off *The Time of Your Life*.

Grayson McCouch (MORGAN WINTHROP) played one of the astronauts who helped Bruce Willis save the world from a deadly meteor in the 1998 summer blockbuster *Armageddon*. Two months later, he turned up on television, playing tobacco farmer Sean Logan on the UPN primetime serial, *Legacy*. *Legacy* was set in Kansas during the late nineteenth century, a time period that has always fascinated the actor.

Grayson McCouch's (MORGAN WINTHROP) career after daytime has taken him into outer space and the nineteenth Century.

© *Barry Morgenstein*

Czaja Carnek is one of those distinctive names like Marcellus Wallace, the *Pulp Fiction* mob boss who made Ving Rhames famous. As Czaja, Rhames kidnapped Cass Winthrop (Stephen Schnetzer) under orders from Queen Cecile (Nancy Frangione). Rhames's cohort in crime, LaRusso, was played by Walt Willey, better known to *All My Children* fans as Jackson Montgomery.

Laura Innes spent the summer of 1988 haunting Cass Winthrop as the ghost of Nora Diamond, a dead ringer for his presumed-dead wife, Kathleen. These days, Innes plays disabled doctor Kerry Weaver on the top-rated drama *ER*. She also starred with Morgan Freeman in the meteor film *Deep Impact*.

Brad Pitt, who starred with Freeman in *Seven*, did day work on the show as a high school student.

Between starring on *General Hospital* and *Northern Exposure*, Janine Turner had a short stint on *Another World* as Scott LaSalle's girlfriend.

Gabrielle Carteris, best known as the bookish Andrea on the Fox prime-time teen serial *Beverly Hills, 90210*, played Tracey Julian, who dated Matt Cory (Matt Crane).

Carteris's future *90210* castmate Luke Perry did day work as Josie's (Alexandra Wilson) manager. Perry and Wilson had worked together the previous year on the ABC soap *Loving*. When Wilson turned up for a summer on *90210*, she was paired not with Perry's Dylan but with Jason Priestley's Brandon.

Rena Sofer, who played ex-con Eve Cleary on *90210*'s sister show *Melrose Place*, played one of Sam Fowler's (Robert Kelker-Kelly) girlfriends.

During the 1960s, Billy Dee Williams (*Lady Sings the Blues*, *The Empire Strikes Back*) played an assistant district attorney.

During a remote shot on Coney Island, a very young Melissa Joan Hart, star of *Sabrina, the Teenage Witch*, was seen rollerskating.

Before Marla Maples's affair with Donald Trump made national headlines, Maples had shown up for an onscreen party on the arm of Jason Frame (Chris Robinson).

Christine Baranski, who won an Emmy playing Cybill Shepherd's best friend in the sitcom *Cybill,* did day work as Beverly Tucker.

When *Frasier* star Kelsey Grammer co-hosted the *Soap Opera Digest* Awards in 1994, the show aired an emergency room clip from his summer as Dr. Canard. At the end of that summer, he joined the cast of *Cheers.*

NICE TO SEE YOU AGAIN

1. What member of the Frame family did Beverlee McKinsey play months before taking on the role of Iris Carrington?
(a) Emma   (b) Sharlene   (c) Janice   (d) Earline

2. Which of the actors who portrayed Sam Fowler had previously played a stalker obsessed with Josie Watts?
(a) Robert Kelker-Kelly   (b) Thomas Gibson
(c) Danny Markel   (d) Brian Lane Green

3. What character did John Considine (REGINALD LOVE) play in the 1970s?
(a) Gerald Davis   (b) Willis Frame
(c) Dr. Dan Shearer   (d) Vic Strang

4. What doctor did John Bolger play a year before taking on the role of police captain Gabe McNamara?
(a) Dr. Alton Spader   (b) Dr. Taylor Benson
(c) Dr. Pressman   (d) Dr. John Hudson

5. What kind of character did Robin Christopher (LORNA DEVON) play when she first appeared on the show as an extra?
   (a) a hospital patient   (b) a dead hooker
   (c) a groupie   (d) a nurse

6. In addition to playing David Thatcher and Ken Jordan, Lewis Arlt has worked in what capacity on the show?
   (a) writer   (b) director   (c) producer   (d) publicist

7. Which of Felicia Gallant's husbands did John Aprea play before coming back as Greek shipping tycoon Alexander Nikos?
   (a) Louis St. George   (b) Zane Lindquist
   (c) Mitch Blake   (d) Lucas Castigliano

8. Gary Carpenter, who played Mike Bauer on *The Guiding Light* and *Another World*, also took over the role of Ray Gordon from what future primetime soap actor?
   (a) John James (JEFF COLBY, *Dynasty*)
   (b) Patrick Duffy (BOBBY EWING, *Dallas*)
   (c) Robert Foxworth (CHASE GIOBERTI, *Falcon Crest*)
   (d) Ted Shackelford (GARY EWING, *Knots Landing*)

9. Which of the actors who played Mike Bauer's brother Ed on *The Guiding Light* also played *Another World*'s Philip Lyons, Cecile de Poulignac's gigolo ex-boyfriend, and Craig Morris, the detective hunting down Dr. Shane Roberts?
   (a) Mart Hulswit   (b) Robert Gentry
   (c) Peter Simon   (d) Richard Van Vleet

10. How many years had passed between the time Robert Kelker-Kelly left the role of Sam Fowler and returned as Bobby Reno a.k.a. Dr. Shane Roberts?
   (a) 3   (b) 6   (c) 9   (d) 12

Famous Fans

IN HER YOUNGER DAYS, movie legend Bette Davis, whose mother followed the radio soaps, thought someone would have to be crazy to watch television in the afternoon. As she got older and her film career cooled down, she got hooked on several of the Procter & Gamble soaps, among them *Another World*. When the character of Walter Curtin was killed off, she telephoned actor Val Dufour to offer her condolences and tell him what a wonderful job he had done those last few days.

Like Davis, legendary singer Lena Horne was a fan of not only the show but of Val Dufour in particular. She spotted him while taking a tour of the studio and admonished him to treat his wife, Lenore, better.

The legendary singer-actress Judy Garland, best known for her performance as Dorothy in *The Wizard of Oz*, was so thrown by seeing Constance Ford (ADA DAVIS) in the audience at one of her concerts that she had to take a break.

The legendary pianist Liberace, known for his outrageous outfits and opulent lifestyle, loved Linda Dano as romance novelist Felicia Gallant. When he played Radio City Music Hall, Liberace sent Dano an invitation. With the producers' permission, Dano asked the showman to make a guest appearance on the soap. He agreed to come on only if he could interact with Felicia and his other favorite character, Wallingford (Brent Collins). Liberace played himself and was revealed to be a reader of Felicia's romance novels. He performed a piano duet with Felicia and wound up with an invitation to her wedding.

Judy Garland was thrown when she saw Constance Ford
(ADA DAVIS) at her concert.

© Robin Platzer, Images

Country singer Crystal Gayle ("Don't It Make My Brown Eyes Blue") has been watching *Another World* since she was a teenager. While on tour, she tunes in when she can. When she can't watch, her sisters fill her in on what she's missed. In 1987, Gayle was offered the chance to not only record the new theme song, but also to perform it on the show. Gayle, who once picked Felicia Gallant as her favorite character, was introduced as a long-time friend of Felicia's. During her onscreen visit, Gayle was targeted for death by the show's resident serial killer, the Sin Stalker.

Blind country musician Ronnie Milsap ("Any Day Now," "Smokey Mountain Rain") was yet another fan who got to perform on the show. Like Gayle, he had been tuning in for decades before making his soap opera debut. He began following the show during his college years when the Rachel/Steve/Alice triangle was at its peak. Although Milsap did not play himself, he did play a musician whom budding record company executive Matthew Cory (Matt Crane) was checking out. When Milsap showed up at the Brooklyn studios, Victoria Wyndham (RACHEL CORY) came out to greet him. As soon as she said, "Hello, Ronnie," he immediately recognized her voice.

RuPaul, the six-foot-plus cross dressing model-singer–talk show host, had never been into *Another World* until Rhonda Ross Kendrick (TONI BURRELL) guested on his VH1 talk show. Afterward, RuPaul checked out the show and took a liking to the six-foot-four-inch Henry Simmons (TYRONE MONTGOMERY), who has since appeared on RuPaul's radio program. The producers, in turn, invited RuPaul to guest on *Another World*. (He had already made a guest appearance on *All My Children*.) A role was even created specifically for him, as a fashion consultant hired to spruce up Cindy Harrison's (Kim Rhodes) image. The appearance didn't work out due to scheduling conflicts.

Whenever talk show host Montell Williams gets the chance, he likes to check out *Another World*, mainly to see what Felicia Gallant (Linda Dano) has been up to. Linda Dano, whom he once picked as his favorite soap performer, has been a guest on his talk show several times.

Actor–calypso singer Harry Belafonte was thrilled when he happened to run into Virginia Dwyer (MARY MATTHEWS) in a television studio. Upon seeing her walk through the door, he began shouting, "Mary Matthews! Mary Matthews!"

Ron Palillo, best known as Arnold Horshack on the 1970s sitcom *Welcome Back, Kotter*, had been tuning into *Another World* since the late '60s. He was immediately drawn into the show when he flicked it on during one of Lee Randolph's (Barbara Rodell) LSD trips. Palillo would have liked to work on the show; he saw enough physical resemblance between himself and Stephen Schnetzer to play Cass's brother or another relative. Although he wasn't hired by *Another World*, he did wind up with a short-term stint on *AW*'s rival for the 2:00 time slot, *One Life to Live*. When his schedule allowed, Palillo would slip away and find a backstage TV where he would watch *Another World*.

Although *Beverly Hills, 90210* star Tori Spelling is mainly a *Days of Our Lives* fan, when she has the time, she will leave the TV on to check out the goings-on in Bay City.

Tennessee Williams, who wrote such theater classics as *A Streetcar Named Desire* and *Cat on a Hot Tin Roof,* counted *Another World* as one of his favorite television series.

Alice Barrett (FRANKIE FRAME) discovered that movie superstar Julia Roberts (*Pretty Woman*, *My Best Friend's Wedding*) is an *Another World* fan. Barrett filled in for Roberts during rehearsals for the series finale of *Murphy Brown,* on which Roberts was a special guest star. When Roberts finally arrived on the set, Barrett was surprised to find that Roberts recognized her as Frankie Frame. After giving Barrett a hug, Roberts admitted that she was thrown for a loop the day that Frankie was killed off.

Cast Members Who Were Fans First

IRENE DAILEY auditioned for the role of Aunt Liz Matthews with Nicolas Coster (ROBERT DELANEY). Before she left the audition, she told Coster that she had followed his career from soap to soap and was hoping to work with him.

Elain M. Graham (ETTA MAE BURRELL) had been watching *Another World* since the early 1970s. She remembered when Victoria Wyndham took over the role of Rachel. After joining the cast and meeting Wyndham, Graham made it a point to talk about the show's old days.

Colleen Dion (BRETT GARDNER), a self confessed "soapaholic," was watching up to five soaps a day, including *Another World*. She joined the cast after leaving *The Bold and the Beautiful*, another soap she watched before joining.

Christine Tucci first checked out the show when she auditioned for the role of Lorna Devon. Even though she didn't get the role, she was hooked on watching the show. By the time she won the part of Amanda Cory, she knew her way around Bay City pretty well.

Amy Carlson (JOSIE WATTS), who had gotten friendly with Tucci on the audition circuit, checked out the show after Tucci mentioned she had landed a role on it. Although not a die-hard fan, Carlson had occasionally tuned in to *Another World* back when she was in high school.

When Dealing with the Public

ROBIN STRASSER was worried about negative fan reaction when Rachel's pregnancy was causing seemingly irreparable damage to the popular relationship between Steve and Alice. Strasser, pregnant in real life as well as on the show, worried not only for herself, but also for the baby she was carrying. Soap fans, Strasser knew, could become physically violent. Eileen Fulton, who played the villainous Lisa Miller on *As the World Turns*, had been slapped in a department store and received such vicious threats that she needed a bodyguard to escort her to and from the studio. Although Strasser did not hire a bodyguard, her then husband, actor Larry Luckinbill, met her at the studio every afternoon to make sure that she made it home safely.

A distant relative noticed Strasser's name in the end credits and placed a call to Robin's mother to see if this Robin Strasser was Martin Strasser's daughter. Robin, who never knew her father, met the woman and through her learned not only about her father's suicide but about his life as well.

Much of Rue McClanahan's screen time as the psychotic nanny Caroline Johnson was spent trying to poison Pat Randolph (Beverly Penberthy). (Caroline was secretly in love with Pat's husband, John.) McClanahan found it amusing that Caroline's poison did nothing more than make Pat sick to her stomach. One fan, frustrated with the story as well, wrote a letter instructing McClanahan on what type of poison she needed to get. In the letter, the woman went on to admit that she had actually used such a poison to kill her present husband's late wife. McClanahan could not tell whether or not the letter was a joke.

When head writer Harding Lemay took a vacation in Ireland, a former fan tracked him down to his hotel. The woman, who had moved to Ireland years before with her husband, missed Bay City and wanted to be brought up to speed. Lemay obliged. (*Another World* was not syndicated to Ireland until years later.)

Every time Steve and Alice announced that they were getting married, one viewer went out to buy a new dress for the wedding. When the two finally tied the knot, hundreds of brides-to-be wrote in wanting to know where Alice had gotten her wedding dress.

One George Reinholt fan literally collapsed after hearing that Steve Frame had been killed in a helicopter crash.

One day while driving on the highway, Victoria Wyndham (RACHEL CORY) was recognized by the woman collecting fares at the tollbooth. "Are you Rachel?" the woman asked. When Wyndham replied that she was, the toll collector said that she had been following the show for years. Just as Wyndham started to drive away, the woman called out, "I can't wait to tell my friends that I met Robin Strasser."

Not wanting to be bothered while she shopped in a department store, Wyndham disguised herself as best she could underneath a big hat, sunglasses, and muffler. As soon as she stepped onto the elevator and asked someone to press the third floor button, all three women on the elevator with her shouted, "Rachel!"

Charles Keating's reign as *Another World*'s pre-eminent, and at times over-the-top, villain has provoked some over-the-top reactions from the show's fans. When Keating would go grocery shopping, patrons who recognized him would fill in other shoppers on Carl's varied misdeeds. And when

Keating took his wife out to a restaurant, fans would warn her what a terrible man she was with.

After Ricky Paull Goldin (DEAN FRAME) performed a concert at his old school, one of the fans became a little too taken with him. She would call the *Another World* studio up to eighty times a day, asking to speak with him. During one of those calls, she mentioned that she had carved Goldin's initials into her thigh. After that revelation, Goldin filed for a restraining order.

Another fan became a little too obsessed with befriending Linda Dano (FELICIA GALLANT). Not only did the young woman find out Dano's home address, she would often stop by to leave notes on the windshield of Dano's car. Once, while cooking dinner, Dano turned around to discover the woman standing inside her kitchen. The incident prompted Dano and her husband to sell their house and move away. Since then, Dano has not been stalked by the woman.

Dano, it should be noted, has become good friends with some of the show's fans. One in particular, Melissa Osorio, had become a regular not only at the *Another World* fan club luncheons but at Dano's talk show *Attitudes* as well. One afternoon, Dano offered Osorio and her friends a ride back to Manhattan in her limousine. Ten minutes after Dano walked in the door, Osorio's mother called to let her know that Melissa had been struck by a cab on her way to the subway station near Dano's apartment. Dano rushed up the street, arriving just as Osorio was being lifted into the ambulance. Explaining that she was a friend, Dano climbed into the ambulance. Just before the ambulance pulled away, it was struck by another cab. Dano waited at the hospital until Osorio's parents were able to arrive. (Osorio underwent surgery and spent a week in the hospital.)

Susan Keith (CECILE DE POULIGNAC) became more than friends with one fan. While she was promoting the show in Toronto, four law students tracked her down at the hotel where she was staying. They showed up at her door, each carrying a bouquet of long-stemmed roses. Charmed by the gesture,

Keith spent some time with the four young men, one of whom became her boyfriend. The two went on a couple of camping trips together, but the distance between New York and Toronto took its toll on the relationship, which lasted only a few months.

Kale Browne (MICHAEL HUDSON) was more than a little taken aback at one promotional event when two girls, no older than thirteen, asked him veiled questions about the size of his penis.

One letter to the producers came from a nurse who worked in a cancer ward. She was writing on behalf of her patients, who were worried about what was going to happen to the various characters. Some of the terminal patients worried that they would never find out. Not wanting to give away upcoming plot details, the producer wrote back instructing the nurse to assure her patients that everything would turn out all right.

One letter Allison Hossack (OLIVIA MATTHEWS) received read like typical fan mail until the last paragraph, in which the writer asked if he and Hossack could wrestle barefoot together sometime.

After John Aprea relocated from California to New York, he was not looking forward to renewing his driver's license. By the time he arrived at the Department of Motor Vehicles, the line was already stretching out the door. One of the people working there recognized him as Lucas and gestured for him to move to the front. Aprea was a little torn. He realized that it wasn't exactly fair for him to skip ahead of all the people who had been waiting, but he also didn't want to stand there another minute. So, as he moved to the front of the line, he mumbled something about having been there earlier in the day.

Kaitlin Hopkins (DR. KELSEY HARRISON) was stopped in the street by one fan who pointed out that she wasn't as pretty in person as she was on television.

One little old lady struck Robert Kelker-Kelly with her purse because she didn't like the way Sam was treating Amanda. As the old lady walked away, she tossed out a couple of nasty remarks.

John Considine's convincing performance as the villainous Reginald Love earned him his share of animated fan reactions. One spat at his feet when she saw him. Another hissed in his face and walked away without saying a word. While walking around a racetrack in Florida with his good friend, movie star Paul Newman, a fan shouted to him, "Hey Reginald, you creep!"—which amused Newman greatly.

B. J. Jefferson (RONNIE LAWRENCE) happened to sit next to a fan in church one Sunday. Not willing to wait until the service ended, the fan talked to Jefferson about the show all through mass. Another time, Jefferson dealt with an over-enthusiastic fan who cornered her in an airport ladies room. Jefferson would not have minded chatting about the varied goings-on in Bay City, except that she had needed to use the restroom urgently and nearly missed her flight.

While Amy Carlson (JOSIE WATTS) was on a rafting trip with a friend, an *Another World* fan approached her to tell her how much she (Carlson) resembled an actress on the show. Carlson's friend informed the fan that Carlson was that same actress. The fan refused to believe it and advised Carlson to check out the show.

Paul Michael Valley (RYAN HARRISON) was taken to a hospital after getting knocked out on the set. (He had fallen backward the wrong way and hit his head on the mantelpiece.) While he lay in the emergency room on a stretcher, a fan came over to see him. The fan asked for an autograph, acknowledging, "I know this is a bad time." Despite being a little out of it, Valley gave her the autograph.

Ray Liotta had one of the more unexpected and more than likely unwelcome instances of recognition back when he was playing Joey Perrini. One afternoon, Liotta had slipped into a peep show in Times Square. As soon as the window in his booth was raised, the stripper looked at him and yelled, "Oh my God. It's Joey Perrini!"

Paul Michael Valley (RYAN HARRISON) has given autographs under the most trying of circumstances. Also pictured: Jensen Buchanan (VICKY HUDSON).
© Barry Morgenstein

JUST PASSING THROUGH TOWN

1. What song did Felicia Gallant (Linda Dano) play with Liberace on his piano?
- (a) "The Wedding March"
- (b) "Tea for Two"
- (c) "Chopsticks"
- (d) "I Could Write a Book"

2. What type of role did talk show host Dick Cavett play when he appeared on the show in 1988?
- (a) an undertaker
- (b) a cab driver
- (c) a magician
- (d) a romance novel ghostwriter

3. Which talk show host visited Felicia Gallant to comfort her friend over Lucas's death in 1993?
- (a) Sally Jessy Raphael
- (b) Oprah Winfrey
- (c) Ricki Lake
- (d) Rosie O'Donnell

4. Which former talk show host showed up at the twenty-fifth anniversary party for Cory Publishing?
   (a) Jack Paar   (b) Virginia Graham
   (c) Steve Allen   (d) Arsenio Hall

5. Which *Today Show* regular played himself in 1990?
   (a) Al Roker   (b) Willard Scott
   (c) Bryant Gumbel   (d) Matt Lauer

6. Which Oscar-winning Best Actor played lawyer Reuben Marino in 1982?
   (a) Art Carney   (b) Lee Marvin
   (c) José Ferrer   (d) Cliff Robertson

7. Which of the following singers has not performed on *Another World*?
   (a) Crystal Gayle   (b) Roberta Flack
   (c) Peabo Bryson   (d) Ronnie Milsap

8. Which Frame sister did screen and TV actress Elizabeth Ashley (*The Carpetbaggers*, *Coma*) play for three months in 1990?
   (a) Sharlene Frame   (b) Emma Ordway
   (c) Gwen Parrish   (d) the ghost of Janice Frame

9. What relationship was Joan Rivers's character Meredith Dunston to Grant and Cindy Harrison?
   (a) She was their marriage counselor.
   (b) She was blackmailing them.
   (c) She was Grant's public relations expert.
   (d) She was Cindy's mother.

10. Which "Golden Girl" played an ex-girlfriend of Mac Cory's?
    (a) Bea Arthur   (b) Betty White
    (c) Rue McClanahan   (d) Estelle Getty

The Daytime Emmy Awards:
WINNERS, NOMINEES, BACKSTAGE STORIES, AND CURIOSITIES

the 1975 DAYTIME EMMY AWARDS
presented May 15, 1975

Head writer Harding Lemay competed in the writing category against *Another World* co-creator Bill Bell, who was double-nominated, once for *Days of Our Lives* and once for *The Young and the Restless*. The awards show producers were so sure that Bell, who held two of the three nominations, would win that the camera was focused on him and not Lemay when the winner's name was announced. Lemay's victory came just days after the recently fired George Reinholt (STEVE FRAME) had insulted Lemay's scripts in a *TV Guide* interview as containing "lifeless, plastic dialogue."

Emmys
Outstanding Writing: Harding Lemay, Tom King, Charles Kozloff,
Jan Merlin, and Doug Marland

Nominations
Outstanding Daytime Drama Series: Paul Rauch (executive producer),
Joe Rothenberger and Mary Bonner (producers)

Outstanding Individual Director: Ira Cirker

the 1976 DAYTIME EMMY AWARDS
presented May 11, 1976

Another World managed to be named Outstanding Daytime Drama Series without racking up a single nomination in any other category. It remains the only time that *Another World* has won the top award. James Luisi, who played Phil Wainwright, picked up the Emmy for Outstanding Actor in a Daytime Drama special for his performance in *First Ladies Diaries: Martha Washington*. He tied for the award with another soap actor, Gerald Gordon (DR. NICK BELLINI, *The Doctors*).

Emmys

Outstanding Daytime Drama Series: Paul Rauch (executive producer), Joe Rothenberger and Mary Bonner (producers)

the 1977 DAYTIME EMMY AWARDS
presented May 12, 1977

Beverlee McKinsey became the first performer to be nominated for an Emmy for *Another World*.

Nominations

Outstanding Daytime Drama Series: Paul Rauch (executive producer), Joe Rothenberger and Mary Bonner (producers)

Outstanding Actress: Beverlee McKinsey (Iris Carrington)

Outstanding Individual Director: Ira Cirker

Outstanding Writing: Harding Lemay, Tom King, Peter Swet, Barry Berg, Jan Merlin, Arthur Giron, and Kathy Callaway

the 1978 DAYTIME EMMY AWARDS
presented June 7, 1978

Seven actresses were vying for the Best Actress Emmy, three from *Another World*—Victoria Wyndham (RACHEL CORY), Beverlee McKinsey (IRIS CARRINGTON), and Laurie Heineman (SHARLENE FRAME), who won. Heineman's victory surprised more than a few insiders. Even her nomination came as a surprise. She had been off the show for more than a year when her name was announced. Only the tail end of her work had taken place during the eligibility period. As for her victory, industry experts believe that Wyndham and McKinsey split the vote, allowing dark horse Heineman to walk away with the trophy. Douglass Watson (MAC CORY) picked up an Emmy for Individual Achievement in Religious Programming for narrating *Continuing Creation*.

Emmys
Outstanding Actress: Laurie Heineman (SHARLENE FRAME)

Nominations
Outstanding Lead Actress: Beverlee McKinsey (IRIS CARRINGTON) and
Victoria Wyndham (RACHEL CORY)

Outstanding Individual Director: Ira Cirker

the 1979 DAYTIME EMMY AWARDS
presented May 17, 1979

Once again, three actresses from *Another World* were competing against one another in the leading actress category, which once again had swelled to seven contenders. Once again, Wyndham and McKinsey lost out to a castmate, this time Irene Dailey, who played Aunt Liz Matthews. Dailey was serving on jury duty the day she learned that she had been nominated as Best Actress. Because jury duty lasted a full month or more in those days, Dailey was pressed for time in putting together her performance reel. One of the associate producers helped her pick out scenes, which she looked over one Saturday morning. Among the scenes that won her the Emmy was a comic moment in which Aunt Liz was gossiping in church.

Irene Dailey (AUNT LIZ MATTHEWS) learned of her Emmy nomination while serving on jury duty.

© Robin Platzer, Images

Emmys

Outstanding Actress: Irene Dailey (Liz Matthews)

Nominations

Outstanding Actress: Beverlee McKinsey (Iris Carrington) and
Victoria Wyndham (Rachel Cory)

Outstanding Direction: Ira Cirker, Melvin Bernhardt, Paul Lammers, and
Robert Calhoun

the 1980 Daytime Emmy Awards
presented June 2 and June 4, 1980

Four nominations without an Emmy seemed to be Beverlee McKinsey's
limit. Only once during her years at *Guiding Light* did she enter her name
for Emmy consideration even though critics praised her portrayal of
Alexandra Spaulding as among the best in daytime. When asked why she
never submitted her name, she would refer back to the four times she had
tried to win as Iris and hadn't. Singer Julius LaRosa, who hosted his own
musical variety series in the 1950s, was one of several celebrities (including Sammy Davis Jr. and Joan Fontaine) who pulled down nominations for
their short-term stints on daytime.

Emmys

Outstanding Actor: Douglass Watson (Mac Cory)

Nominations

Outstanding Daytime Drama Series: Paul Rauch (executive producer),
Joe Rothenberger and Mary Bonner (producers)

Outstanding Actress: Beverlee McKinsey (Iris Carrington)

Outstanding Supporting Actor: Julius LaRosa (Renaldo)

Outstanding Direction: Ira Cirker, Melvin Bernhardt, Robert Calhoun,
Barnet Kellman, and Andrew Weyman

the 1981 DAYTIME EMMY AWARDS

presented May 19 and 21, 1981

The year 1981 saw the same two performers, Douglass Watson (MAC CORY) and Judith Light (KAREN WOLEK, *One Life to Live*), walk away with the Best Actor and Actress Emmys for the second year in a row. After leaving his head-writing position on *Another World*, Harding Lemay went to work for *Guiding Light*'s Doug Marland, whom Lemay had given his first job writing for a soap. Lemay had also helped Marland win his first Emmy for writing; Marland repaid the favor by helping Lemay win his second.

Emmys

Outstanding Actor: Douglass Watson (MAC CORY)

the 1982 DAYTIME EMMY AWARDS

presented June 8, 1982

For the first time since 1974, *Another World* did not garner any nominations in the acting, writing, or directing categories.

the 1983 DAYTIME EMMY AWARDS

presented June 6, 1983

Howard E. Rollins (ED HARDING) was nominated for an Emmy in the category Best Supporting Actor in 1983. One year previously he had been nominated for an Oscar in the same category for his work in the film *Ragtime*.

Nominations

Outstanding Supporting Actor: Howard E. Rollins Jr. (ED HARDING)

the 1984 DAYTIME EMMY AWARDS
presented June 27, 1984

Many people attending the ceremony knew in advance that Paul Stevens (BRIAN BANCROFT) was not going to win the Emmy. The *New York Post*, which had been given an advance list of the winners, published the results in its afternoon edition, which came out before the awards ceremony had even begun.

Nominations

Outstanding Supporting Actor: Paul Stevens (BRIAN BANCROFT)

the 1985 DAYTIME EMMY AWARDS
presented August 1, 1985

Gillian Spencer, who was head-writing *Another World* at the time, picked up an Emmy nomination as Best Actress for her work on the ABC soap opera *All My Children*.

Nominations

Outstanding Writing: Gary Tomlin, Samuel D. Ratcliffe, Richard Culliton, Carolyn Culliton, Judith Donato, David Cherrill, Judith Pinsker, Frances Myers, Roger Newman, Lloyd Gold, and Cynthia Saltzman

the 1986 DAYTIME EMMY AWARDS
presented July 17, 1986

Some critics called 1986 the Year of the Twin. Ellen Wheeler won the Best Ingenue Emmy for playing Marley and Vicky Love; and David Canary, who played Steve Frame a couple years earlier, picked up the Best Actor Emmy for his work as twins Stuart and Adam Chandler. Wheeler, who was leaving *Another World* when she won her Emmy, headed over to *All My Children*, where she was paired up with Canary. Their work on an AIDS storyline would earn them each another Emmy.

Emmys

Outstanding Ingenue: Ellen Wheeler (VICKY and MARLEY LOVE)

Nominations

Outstanding Younger Leading Man: Don Scardino (DR. CHRIS CHAPIN)

the 1987 DAYTIME EMMY AWARDS

presented June 30, 1987

and the 1988 DAYTIME EMMY AWARDS

presented June 29, 1988

Another World hit a dry spell in the late 1980s, going two years without receiving a single nomination in the acting, writing, or directing categories.

the 1989 DAYTIME EMMY AWARDS

presented June 29, 1989

Douglass Watson (MAC CORY) died shortly after being nominated as Best Actor. Linda Dano received her first Emmy nomination, but not for *Another World*. She was nominated as Outstanding Talk/Service Show Host for her work on *Attitudes*.

Emmys

Outstanding Costume Design

Nominations

Outstanding Lead Actor: Doug Watson (MAC CORY)

Outstanding Supporting Actor: David Forsyth (DR. JOHN HUDSON)

Outstanding Juvenile Female: Anne Heche (VICKY and MARLEY LOVE)

Outstanding Writing: Donna Swajeski, Chris Whitesell, David Colson, Roger Newman, Fran Myers, and Carolyn Culliton

the 1990 DAYTIME EMMY AWARDS

presented June 28, 1990

Another World shared its Emmy for costume design with *All My Children*—one of the very few times that two soaps tied for an Emmy.

Emmys

Outstanding Costume Design (tied with *All My Children*)

Outstanding Hairstyling

Nominations

Outstanding Lead Actor: Stephen Schnetzer (CASS WINTHROP)

the 1991 DAYTIME EMMY AWARDS

presented June 27, 1991

Just like her predecessor Ellen Wheeler, Anne Heche picked up the Younger Actress Emmy for playing Vicky and Marley as she was on her way out the door. She had already taped her last episode of *Another World* and was off filming a TV movie, which kept her from attending the 1991 awards ceremony. Procter & Gamble, which owns *Another World* as well as a slew of soaps past and present, became the first and as yet only nonperson to be presented with a Lifetime Achievement Award in 1991.

Emmys

Outstanding Younger Actress: Anne Heche (VICKY and MARLEY HUDSON)

the 1992 DAYTIME EMMY AWARDS

presented June 23, 1992

NBC preceded the awards ceremony with a special primetime episode of *Another World.*

Outstanding Directing Team: Janet Andrews, Casey Childs,
Michael Eilbaum, Mary Madeiras, Bob Schwarz, and Carol Sedwick

Emmys
Outstanding Hairstyling

Nominations
Outstanding Supporting Actor: Charles Keating (CARL HUTCHINS)

Outstanding Supporting Actress: Linda Dano (FELICIA GALLANT)

Outstanding Younger Actress: Alla Korot (JENNA NORRIS)

the 1993 DAYTIME EMMY AWARDS
presented May 26, 1993

When John Aprea (LUCAS CASTIGLIANO) was deciding whether or not to
leave the show in 1992, he was upset not only about his own character's
lack of storyline but also about the way the show was neglecting his leading lady and good friend Linda Dano (FELICIA GALLANT). He predicted that
if he left, Dano would end up with an Emmy award—and she did. Lucas's
death propelled Felicia into an alcoholism storyline that netted Dano the
Daytime Emmy for Best Actress.

Emmys
Outstanding Lead Actress: Linda Dano (FELICIA GALLANT)

Outstanding Hairstyling

Nominations
Outstanding Supporting Actor: Charles Keating (CARL HUTCHINS)

Outstanding Directing Team: Janet Andrews, Casey Childs, Michael
Eilbaum, Mary Madeiras, Bob Schwarz, Susan Strickler, and Carol Sedwick

the 1994 DAYTIME EMMY AWARDS
presented May 25, 1994

Another World was nominated for the Outstanding Writing Team award but was disqualified from competing after the wrong reel was sent to the review panel. Instead of a reel containing two complete episodes, the panel received a reel containing highlight clips. Executive producer Terry Guaneri complained that the show should have been allowed the chance to correct its mistake.

Emmys
Outstanding Makeup

Outstanding Hairstyling

Outstanding Costume Design

Nominations
Outstanding Lead Actor: Charles Keating (CARL HUTCHINS)

Outstanding Lead Actress: Linda Dano (FELICIA GALLANT)

Outstanding Writing Team: Peggy Sloane, Peter Brash, Lorraine Broderick, Craig Carlson, Sharon Epstein, Kathleen Kennedy, Kathleen Klein, Mimi Leahy, Victor Miller, Elizabeth Page, Judith Pinsker, Sam Ratcliffe, and Janet Stampfl

the 1995 DAYTIME EMMY AWARDS
presented May 19, 1995

The ceremony was co-hosted by talk show host Leeza Gibbons and *Days of Our Lives* stars Deidre Hall and Robert Kelker-Kelly. Kelker-Kelly was then playing Bo Brady on *Days* but would head back to *Another World*, where he had originated the role of Sam Fowler, the following year.

Emmys

Outstanding Musical Direction and Composition

Outstanding Song: "I Never Believed in Love" by A. J. Gundel and
Gloria Sklerov

Nominations

Outstanding Directing Team: Janet Andrews, Michael Eilbaum,
Lina Laundra, Mary Madeiras, Bob Schwarz, and Carol Sedwick

the 1996 DAYTIME EMMY AWARDS

presented May 22, 1996

Anna Holbrook (SHARLENE FRAME) won the Emmy as Best Supporting Actress
eighteen years after Laurie Heineman won the Best Actress Emmy for playing the same character, making Sharlene Frame one of the few roles on
daytime to have earned Emmys for more than one performer. Holbrook's
castmate Charles Keating took home the gold as Best Actor. Proving that
Emmys do not ensure job security, both Holbrook and Keating were subsequently written off the show, Holbrook in 1997 and Keating in 1998.

Emmys

Outstanding Lead Actor: Charles Keating (CARL HUTCHINS)

Outstanding Supporting Actress: Anna Holbrook
(SHARLENE FRAME HUDSON)

Nominations

Outstanding Lead Actress: Jensen Buchanan (VICKY HUDSON) and
Linda Dano (FELICIA GALLANT)

Outstanding Supporting Actor: David Forsyth (DR. JOHN HUDSON)

Outstanding Writing Team: Carolyn Culliton, Craig Carlson,
Victor Miller, Samuel D. Ratcliffe, Lorraine Broderick, Shelly Altman,
Peter Brash, Mel Brez, Kathy Ebel, Sharon Epstein, Sofia Landon Geier,
Janet Iacobuzio, Kathleen Kennedy, Tom King, Mimi Leahy,
Elisabeth Page, Harding Lemay, Michelle Poteet Lisanti, Loren Segan,
Betsy Snyder, and Christopher Whitesell

the 1997 DAYTIME EMMY AWARDS

presented May 21, 1997

Jensen Buchanan received her second Best Actress nomination. Vicky Hudson, it should be noted, is the only soap opera character to generate Emmy nominations for three different performers. Ellen Wheeler, who created the role, and Anne Heche, who preceded Buchanan, each won Outstanding Ingenue/Younger Actress Emmys for portraying Vicky and her twin sister, Marley. Although Buchanan played both twins in the past, she has been Emmy-nominated only for her work as Vicky.

Nominations

Outstanding Lead Actress: Jensen Buchanan (VICKY HUDSON)

Anna Holbrook (SHARLENE FRAME HUDSON) won an Emmy and was fired a year later.

© *Barry Morgenstein*

the 1998 DAYTIME EMMY AWARDS

presented May 15, 1998

Talk show host Leeza Gibbons co-hosted the 1998 awards ceremony with an actor from each of the three NBC soaps. Joseph Barbara (JOE CARLINO) represented *Another World*.

Nominations

Outstanding Supporting Actress: Amy Carlson (JOSIE WATTS)

Outstanding Younger Actress: Rhonda Ross Kendrick (TONI BURRELL)

the 1999 DAYTIME EMMY AWARDS

presented May 21, 1999

Another World was not nominated for any Emmys in the acting, writing, or directing categories. In addition to the lack of awards, fans were also disappointed that the ceremony did not officially recognize the show's passing.

The Soap Opera Digest Awards:
WINNERS AND NOMINEES

OVER THE YEARS, the *Soap Opera Digest* Awards have been called the Soapys, the *Soap Opera Digest* Awards and, most recently, the Soap Opera Awards. Some critics of the show have also dubbed the ceremony the *Days of Our Lives* Fan Club Awards—a jab at the fact that *Days* has won the lion's share of statuettes over the years. Since 1984, *Days of Our Lives* has tended to win almost every award for which it has been nominated. Before that, *General Hospital* ruled the awards. *Another World*, in fact, did not receive a single award between 1979 and 1983. Fueling the dissension against *Days* have been stories of fan club members bloc voting on awards to ensure that certain performers win the prize. In an effort to more evenly distribute the awards, the editors have changed the voting procedure. In the beginning, the magazine's readers would simply vote for whomever they wanted in each category; in some years the runners-up were listed. Now the list of nominees, chosen by the editors, has been trimmed down to a maximum of three per category.

Jensen Buchanan, whom *Soap Opera Digest* named Worst Recast of the Year when she took over the role of Vicky and Marley Love, has certainly won the editors over since then. In the past five years, she has been nominated for four awards (three as Hottest Female star, and one as Leading Actress). The role also won the 1986 Outstanding Young Lead Actress award for Ellen Wheeler, who originated the role, and a pair of awards for Buchanan's immediate predecessor, Anne Heche—Outstanding Female Newcomer in 1989 and Outstanding Lead Actress in 1992. The dual roles of Vicky and Marley remain the only roles to have earned *Soap Opera Digest* Awards for three different performers. This past year, when the twins were played by separate performers, they each earned a nomination, Buchanan for Hottest Female Performer and Wheeler for Best Return.

Among the actresses Heche beat out for that second trophy was Beverlee McKinsey, who was then nominated for her work on *Guiding Light*. It was for her portrayal of Iris Carrington on *Another World*, however, that McKinsey picked up back-to-back *Soap Opera Digest* Awards for Best Villainess (1977 and 1978). She was, in fact, the first performer to win back-to-back *Soap Opera Digest* Awards.

Ten-time nominee Tom Eplin (Jake McKinnon).
© *Albert Ortega, Moonglow Photos*

Heche, McKinsey, and Tom Eplin (JAKE McKINNON) are the only performers from *Another World* to win more than one trophy. Eplin was voted Outstanding Actor in 1995 and Outstanding Male Showstopper in 1997. Eplin also holds the record as *Another World's* most-nominated performer. He has racked up ten nominations since 1986, when the magazine's editors started selecting nominees. In addition to Leading Actor and Showstopper, he's been nominated as Young Leading Actor, Supporting Actor, Villain, and Hottest Male Star.

Bill Bell, who co-created *Another World*, and Agnes Nixon, whose head-writing saved it from cancellation in the 1960s, have each received two Editors Awards for their contributions to daytime television.

Nancy Frangione (CECILE DE POULIGNAC) was named
Outstanding Villianess in 1984.

© *Barry Morgenstein*

the 1977 SOAPY AWARDS

Favorite Villainess: Beverlee McKinsey (IRIS CARRINGTON)

the 1978 SOAPY AWARDS

Favorite Actress: Victoria Wyndham (RACHEL CORY)

Favorite Villain: Roberts Blossom (SVEN PETERSEN)

Favorite Villainess: Beverlee McKinsey (IRIS CARRINGTON)

the 1984 *SOAP OPERA DIGEST* AWARDS

Outstanding Villainess: Nancy Frangione (CECILE DE POULIGNAC)

Outstanding Youth Actor in a Daytime Soap,
1st Runner-Up: Trevor Richard (KEVIN THATCHER)

Outstanding Actor in a Mature Role,
2nd Runner-Up: Douglass Watson (MAC CORY)

the 1985 *SOAP OPERA DIGEST* AWARDS

Outstanding Villain, 4th place: Charles Keating (CARL HUTCHINS)

Outstanding Villainess, 4th place:
Nancy Frangione (CECILE DE POULIGNAC)

Outstanding Actor in a Mature Role, 3rd place:
Douglass Watson (MAC CORY)

Outstanding Actress in a Mature Role, 5th place:
Constance Ford (ADA HOBSON)

Outstanding Youth Actor, 3rd place: Trevor Richard (KEVIN THATCHER)

the 1986 SOAP OPERA DIGEST AWARDS
Winners
Outstanding Young Leading Actress: Ellen Wheeler
(MARLEY and VICKY LOVE)

Nominees
Outstanding Actor in a Supporting Role: Russell Curry (CARTER TODD)

Outstanding Young Leading Actor: Tom Eplin (JAKE MCKINNON)

Outstanding Comic Relief: Stephen Schnetzer (CASS WINTHROP)

Outstanding Contribution by an Actor/Actress to the Form of
Continuing Drama Who Is Currently on a Daytime Serial:
Victoria Wyndham (RACHEL CORY)

the 1988 SOAP OPERA DIGEST AWARDS
Nominees
Outstanding Hero: Kale Browne (MICHAEL HUDSON)

Outstanding Villain: John Considine (REGINALD LOVE) and
Marcus Smythe (PETER LOVE)

Outstanding Newcomer: Hank Cheyne (SCOTT LASALLE)

the 1989 SOAP OPERA DIGEST AWARDS
Winners
Outstanding Female Newcomer: Anne Heche (VICKY and MARLEY LOVE)

Outstanding Comic Actor: Stephen Schnetzer (CASS WINTHROP)

Nominees
Outstanding Comic Actress: Linda Dano (FELICIA GALLANT)

the 1990 *Soap Opera Digest* Awards

Nominees

Outstanding Supporting Actor: Tom Eplin (JAKE MCKINNON) and David Forsyth (DR. JOHN HUDSON)

Outstanding Villain: Chris Robinson (JASON FRAME)

Outstanding Female Newcomer: Carmen Duncan (IRIS CARRINGTON WHEELER)

the 1991 *Soap Opera Digest* Awards

Nominees

Outstanding Supporting Actor: Stephen Schnetzer (CASS WINTHROP)

the 1992 *Soap Opera Digest* Awards

Winners

Outstanding Lead Actress: Anne Heche (VICKY and MARLEY LOVE)

Outstanding Younger Leading Actor: Ricky Paull Goldin (DEAN FRAME)

Outstanding Male Newcomer: Paul Michael Valley (RYAN HARRISON)

Outstanding Female Newcomer: Alla Korot (JENNA NORRIS)

Nominees

Outstanding Lead Actor: Stephen Schnetzer (CASS WINTHROP)

Outstanding Villain: Tom Eplin (JAKE MCKINNON) and Charles Keating (CARL HUTCHINS)

Outstanding Villainess: Carmen Duncan (IRIS CARRINGTON WHEELER)

Best Wedding: Cass and Frankie

Best Love Story: The Frankie/Cass/Kathleen love triangle

the 1993 *SOAP OPERA DIGEST* AWARDS

Winners

Outstanding Younger Leading Actress: Alicia Coppola (LORNA DEVON)

Nominees

Hottest Male Star: Tom Eplin (JAKE McKINNON)

Hottest Female Star: Judi Evans (PAULINA CORY)

Outstanding Supporting Actress: Linda Dano (FELICIA GALLANT)

Outstanding Male Newcomer: Chris Bruno (DENNIS WHEELER)

Outstanding Female Newcomer: Kaitlin Hopkins (KELSEY HARRISON)

Outstanding Villain/Villainess: Charles Keating (CARL HUTCHINS)

Favorite Song: "You Are So Beautiful to Me" (Sam and Amanda's theme)

the 1994 *SOAP OPERA DIGEST* AWARDS

Nominees

Outstanding Lead Actor: Tom Eplin (JAKE McKINNON)

Hottest Male Star: Paul Michael Valley (RYAN HARRISON)

Hottest Female Star: Jensen Buchanan (VICKY and MARLEY LOVE)

Outstanding Supporting Actress: Anna Stuart (DONNA LOVE)

Outstanding Villain/Villainess: Charles Keating (CARL HUTCHINS)

Outstanding Younger Leading Actress: Alicia Coppola (LORNA DEVON)

Outstanding Scene Stealer: Robyn Griggs (MAGGIE CORY)

Favorite Storyline: The Ryan/Vicky/Grant triangle

Outstanding Musical Achievement

the 1995 *SOAP OPERA DIGEST* AWARDS

Winners

Outstanding Lead Actor: Tom Eplin (JAKE McKINNON)

Nominees

Outstanding Supporting Actress: Anna Stuart (DONNA LOVE)

Outstanding Younger Lead Actor: Matt Crane (MATT CORY)

Outstanding Female Newcomer: Amy Carlson (JOSIE WATTS)

Outstanding Male Scene Stealer: Charles Keating (CARL HUTCHINS)

the 1996 *SOAP OPERA DIGEST* AWARDS

Winners

Outstanding Villain: Mark Pinter (GRANT HARRISON)

Nominees

Outstanding Lead Actor: Tom Eplin (JAKE McKINNON)

Hottest Female Star: Jensen Buchanan (VICKY LOVE)

Outstanding Supporting Actor: Timothy Gibbs (GARY SINCLAIR)

Outstanding Female Scene Stealer: Anna Stuart (DONNA LOVE)

the 1997 *SOAP OPERA DIGEST* AWARDS

Winners

Outstanding Male Showstopper: Tom Eplin (JAKE McKINNON)

Nominees

Outstanding Lead Actress: Jensen Buchanan (VICKY LOVE)

Outstanding Supporting Actress: Anna Holbrook (SHARLENE FRAME)

Outstanding Villain: Mark Pinter (GRANT HARRISON)

Hottest Romance: Gary and Josie
(played by Timothy Gibbs and Amy Carlson)

the 1998 *SOAP OPERA DIGEST* AWARDS
Winners
Outstanding Supporting Actress: Judi Evans Luciano
(PAULINA CORY CARLINO)

Nominees
Outstanding Lead Actor: Tom Eplin (JAKE MCKINNON)

Outstanding Male Scene Stealer: Eric Morgan Stuart (CHRIS MADISON)

Favorite New Couple: Grant and Cindy
(played by Mark Pinter and Kim Rhodes)

the 1999 *SOAP OPERA DIGEST* AWARDS
Nominees
Outstanding Lead Actor: Tom Eplin (JAKE MCKINNON)

Hottest Female Star: Jensen Buchanan (VICKY HUDSON MCKINNON)

Outstanding Male Scene Stealer: Stephen Schnetzer (CASS WINTHROP)

Favorite Veteran: Linda Dano (FELICIA GALLANT)

Favorite Return: Ellen Wheeler (MARLEY HUDSON)

1964

In what city did Pat Matthews undergo her illegal abortion?

(a) New York   (b) Milwaukee   (c) Chicago   (d) Detroit

1965

How did Lee Randolph interrupt her father John's honeymoon with Pat?

(a) She came down with pneumonia.

(b) She was arrested for drunk driving.

(c) She called and told them that Pat's mother was sick.

(d) She attempted suicide.

1966

What revelation prompted Missy Palmer to run away right before she was to marry Bill Matthews?

(a) Bill's mother rigged a test to make Missy believe she was dying.

(b) Lenore lied that she was pregnant by Bill.

(c) Missy learned that she was illegitimate.

(d) Missy discovered that she could never have children.

1967

Which character was named Miss Citrus Fruit of 1967?

(a) Rachel Davis   (b) Lahoma Vane

(c) Missy Palmer   (d) Lee Randolph

1968

What drug caused Lee Randolph's fatal car crash?

(a) speed   (b) heroin   (c) cocaine   (d) LSD

1969

Why did Missy Palmer Matthews return to town without her husband Bill?

(a) He was killed in a boating accident.

(b) He had left her for another woman.

(c) She had left him because of his drinking problem.

(d) She was suffering from amnesia.

1970

Why did Walter Curtin kill Wayne Addison?

(a) Walter's wife Lenore had been sleeping with Wayne.

(b) Wayne lied that Lenore had been sleeping with him.

(c) Wayne had raped Lenore.

(d) Wayne had tried to rape Lenore.

1971

Who kidnapped the Randolph twins, Michael and Marianne?

(a) Liz Matthews   (b) Danny Fargo

(c) Caroline Johnson   (d) Steve Frame

1972

What caused Alice Matthews's miscarriage?

(a) Rachel pushed her down a flight of stairs.

(b) She developed food poisoning.

(c) She fell off a step ladder.

(d) She was run down by a drunken Lenore Curtin.

1973

Before Iris Carrington even met Rachel, with which other female was she locking horns?

(a) Alice Matthews   (b) Lenore Curtin

(c) Janice Frame   (d) Pat Randolph

1974

For what crime did Steve Frame go to prison?

    (a) kidnapping Jamie

    (b) bribing Rachel's father to commit perjury during Jamie's custody trial

    (c) bribing a government official to grant him construction contracts

    (d) burning down his own building for the insurance money

1975

In what country was Steve Frame presumably killed in a helicopter crash?

    (a) Australia   (b) Bolivia   (c) Chile   (d) Denmark

1976

How did Sharlene Frame try to kill herself after confessing her past as a prostitute to husband Russ Matthews?

    (a) She sat in the garage with the car running.

    (b) She drove her car into the river.

    (c) She took an overdose of sleeping pills.

    (d) She took a handful of penicillin tablets, to which she was highly allergic.

1977

What event triggered Ada's depression?

    (a) Her husband Gil was killed in an explosion.

    (b) Gil left her for Olive Gordon.

    (c) Her daughter Rachel slept with Gil.

    (d) Her daughter Nancy was diagnosed with a terminal illness.

1978

In what part of the Cory estate did Sven Peterson keep Rachel hostage?

    (a) the pool house   (b) the stables

    (c) the wine cellar   (d) the pump house

1979

Why did Iris encourage Cecile's interest in her (Iris's) son Dennis?

(a) Iris wanted to break up the relationship between Dennis and Cecile's mother.

(b) Iris wanted to keep Cecile away from Russ Matthews.

(c) After being disowned by Mac, Iris wanted Dennis to live off Cecile's fortune.

(d) Iris suspected that Dennis might be gay.

1980

What side effect did the poison Janice Frame used to kill Mac have on him?

(a) It left him blind.   (b) It left him deaf.

(c) It left him sterile.   (d) It gave him amnesia.

1981

Who went on trial for the murder of crooked casino owner Jordan Scott?

(a) Alice Matthews   (b) Blaine Ewing

(c) Cecile de Poulignac   (d) Sally Frame

1982

For what crime did Mitch Blake go to prison?

(a) the attempted murder of Mac Cory

(b) kidnapping his son Matthew

(c) art theft

(d) arson

1983

Why did Felicia Gallant take a waitressing job at Smiley's Diner?

(a) to get closer to Zane Lindquist

(b) to spy on Cass and Cecile

(c) to research her next novel

(d) because her ex-husband Louis St. George had left her penniless

1984

Of what country did Cecile de Poulignac become Queen?

(a) Quitam (b) Tanquir (c) Dudaq (d) Masqiit

1985

On what did Nancy McGowan get hooked?

(a) amphetamines   (b) barbiturates

(c) cocaine   (d) the designer drug Ecstasy

1986

In a sad twist of irony, Sally Spencer died in the same way that her parents had eleven years previously. How did she die?

(a) in a plane crash   (b) in a fire

(c) in a car crash   (d) in a bank holdup

1987

Who did Donna Love fear might be the father of her twins?

(a) Carl Hutchins   (b) John Hudson

(c) Cass Winthrop   (d) her own father Reginald

1988

On what kind of table did Jamie Frame and Vicky Hudson make love for the first time?

(a) a kitchen table in the Frame farmhouse

(b) a drafting table at Frame Construction

(c) an operating table at Bayside General

(d) a boardroom table at Cory Publishing

1989

To whom did Mac's will leave Cory Publishing?

(a) Rachel (b) Iris (c) Amanda (d) all three women

1990

From what kind of animal did Ryan Harrison rescue Vicky Hudson when they first met?

(a) snake   (b) horse   (c) shark   (d) Doberman pinscher

1991

After learning that his wife Kathleen did not die in a plane crash, Cass Winthrop came face to face with her in what city? (Hint: It was where they honeymooned.)

(a) New York   (b) New Orleans   (c) San Francisco   (d) Las Vegas

1992

What record company fired Dean Frame for not living up to his contract?

(a) Ace Records   (b) Brigade Records

(c) Cottonwood Records   (d) Diamond Needle Records

1993

For what crime did Morgan Winthrop go on trial?

(a) rape   (b) blackmail

(c) attempted murder   (d) selling prescriptions

1994

Cass Winthrop was treated for what mental disorder?

(a) agoraphobia   (b) sex addiction

(c) multiple personality disorder   (d) manic depression

1995

What character nearly walked into his own funeral?

(a) Jake McKinnon   (b) Grant Harrison

(c) Ryan Harrison   (d) Carl Hutchins

1996.

How did Grant Harrison get out of prison early when he was convicted of killing Ryan?

(a) Grant blackmailed the governor into giving him a pardon.

(b) The governor pardoned Grant after he saved his daughter's life during a fire.

(c) Grant agreed to test an experimental drug in exchange for an early parole.

(d) The FBI got Grant his pardon in exchange for information he had on Carl Hutchins.

1997

What did Lila Roberts have a talent for forging?

(a) artwork   (b) handwriting   (c) passports   (d) steel

1998

Which of Felicia Gallant's novels came to life?

(a) *Sands of the Desert*   (b) *Handmaiden's Heart*

(c) *Castle of Desire*   (d) *Embers in the Snow*

1999

What is the name of Jordan Stark's mind-controlling foundation?

(a) Alpha/Omega   (b) Infinity   (c) Lumina   (d) Starkbucks

Bonus

Approximately how many episodes of *Another World* aired?

(a) 6,000   (b) 9,000   (c) 12,000   (d) 15,000

Cast List

Abaire, Chris Lindsay	FIONA MERRIMAN
Ackroyd,David	DAVE GILCHRIST
Adams, Mason	FRANK PRESCOTT
Alaio, Rose	ARIANNE
Albee, Denny	DREW MARSTEN
Alexander, Benjamin	MIKEY MILLER
Alexander, Denise	MARY MCKINNON
Alexander, Terry	ZACK RICHARDS
Allen, Elizabeth	VICTORIA BELLMAN
Allen, Vera	GRANDMA MATTHEWS
Allport, Christopher	TIM MCGOWAN
Anderson, John	MIKEY MILLER
Andreas, Christine	TAYLOR BENSON
Andrews, William	GEORGE FENTON
Anthony, Gerald	RICK MADISON
Anthony, Terrell	JOE BARRON
Aprea, John	LUCAS CASTIGLIANO and ALEXANDER NIKOS
Arlt, Lewis	KEN JORDAN and DAVID THATCHER
Arrants, Rod	AUSTIN CUSHING
Ashley, Elizabeth	EMMA FRAME ORDWAY
Backus, Richard	TED BANCROFT
Bailey, David	RUSS MATTHEWS

Bamford, George	SERGEANT HAWKINS
Baranski, Christine	BEVERLY TUCKER
Barbara, Joseph	JOE CARLINO
Barcroft, Judith	LENORE MOORE
Barker, Margaret	LEUEEN PARRISH
Baron, Evalyn	MISS DEVON
Barrett, Alice	FRANKIE FRAME and ANNE O'DONNELL
Barrientos, Marie	PILARA SANCHEZ
Barton, Steve	BAILEY THOMPSON
Bartram, Laurie	KAREN CAMPBELL
Baxter, Charles	FRED DOUGLAS
Beal, John	JIM MATTHEWS
Bedford, Brad	JAMIE FRAME
Beir, Fred	KEITH MORRISON
Beirne, Jeanne	MARIANNE RANDOLPH
Bekins, Richard	JAMIE FRAME
Belack, Doris	MADGE MURRAY
Bell, Joy	CAROLINE STAFFORD
Bellaver, Harry	ERNIE DOWNS
Bellin, Olga	ANN FULLER
Benz, Dawn	SALLY FRAME
Berjer, Barbara	BRIDGET CONNELL
Betts, Jack	LOUIS ST. GEORGE
Biendie, Irene	ELLEN
Bikel, Theodore	HENRY DAVENPORT
Birney, Reed	WALTER TRASK
Blackburn, Dorothy	LUELLA WATSON
Bliss, Bradley	KIT HALLOWAY PERRINI
Bloch, Scotty	CLARA HUDSON
Blossom, Roberts	BERT ORDWAY and SVEN PETERSEN

Blythewood, Reggie Rock	R. J. MORGAN
Bogardus, Stephen	SANDY CORY
Bolger, John	DR. ALTON SPADER and GABE MCNAMARA
Bolster, Stephen	TED CLARK
Bonarrigo, Laura	LINDSEY
Borgeson, Linda	ALICE MATTHEWS
Bowen, Alex	GREGORY HUDSON
Braden, John	ROCKY OLSEN
Brandon, Jane Alice	HARRIET SULLIVAN
Brandt, Les	RAFAEL SANTIERO
Braniff, Blakely	HANNAH MOORE
Brennen, John H.	TONY CARLISLE
Brenner, Lisa	MAGGIE CORY
Brookes, Jacqueline	BEATRICE GORDON
Brooks, Anne Rose	DIANA FRAME
Brooks, Randy	MARSHALL LINCOLN KRAMER III
Brown, Brandy	ANGELA CORELLI
Brown, Chris J.	MICHAEL RANDOLPH
Brown, Gail	CLARICE EWING
Brown, Tracey	MARIANNE RANDOLPH
Browne, Kale	MICHAEL HUDSON
Bruno, Chris	DENNIS WHEELER
Bruns, Mona	EMILY HASTINGS
Bryce, Ed	PHILIP LESSNER
Buchanan, Jensen	VICKY and MARLEY HUDSON
Burgi, Richard	CHAD ROLLO
Burns, Danielle	NANCY MCGOWAN
Burton, Warren	JASON DUNLAP
Bush, Barbara	DAWN ROLLO
Butler, David	BEN CAMPBELL

Cabalero, Roxann	ADRIENNE MORROW
Cameron, Christine	BARBARA SHEARER
Cameron, Jane	NANCY McGOWAN
Cameron, Lisa	SUSAN MATTHEWS
Campbell, Alan	EVAN GRANT
Campbell, J. Kenneth	JORDAN SCOTT
Canary, David	STEVE FRAME
Carlson, Amy	JOSIE WATTS
Carpenter, Gary a.k.a. Gary Pillar	MIKE BAUER and RAYMOND GORDON
Carr, Camilla	RITA CONNELLY
Carrigan, Kevin	DEREK DANE
Carteris, Gabrielle	TRACEY JULIAN
Cassidy, Orlagh	SLOAN WALLACE
Cassmore, Judy	MARGO GROVE
Catalanotto, Nicole	AMANDA CORY
Chambers, Justin	NICK HUDSON
Chapman, Liza	JANET MATTHEWS
Charney, Jordan	SAM LUCAS
Cheyne, Hank	SCOTT LaSALLE
Chon, Bok Yun	LILY TRAN
Christian, Robert	BOB MORGAN
Christopher, Robin	LORNA DEVON
Cioffi, Charles	KIRK LAVERTY
Clanton, Ralph	JASPER DELANEY
Clark, Josh	BERT KELLER
Clark, Spencer Treat	STEVEN FRAME
Coburn, Drew	BARRY DURRELL
Collins, Beth	MARIANNE RANDOLPH
Collins, Brent	WALLINGFORD

Combs, David	BILL GORMAN
Congdon, James	ALEX GREGORY
Conger, Eric	BUZZ WINSLOW
Conroy, Christopher	STEVEN FRAME
Conroy, Kevin	JERRY GROVE
Considine, John	VIC HASTINGS and REGINALD LOVE
Coppola, Alicia	LORNA DEVON
Corwin, Chris	MICHAEL RANDOLPH
Coster, Nicolas	ROBERT DELANEY
Court, Geraldine	JUNE LAVERTY
Courtney, Jacqueline	ALICE MATTHEWS
Cousins, Christopher	GREG HOUSTON
Crane, Matt	MATTHEW CORY
Crawford, John	JOHN BRADFORD
Creech, Cassandra	DANA KRAMER
Crowell, McLin	PHIL HIGLEY
Culp, Jason	TONY CARLINO
Cummings, Tony	RICK HALLOWAY
Cunningham, John	DAN SHEARER
Cunningham, Sarah	LIZ MATTHEWS
Curry, Russell	CARTER TODD
Dabney, Augusta	LAURA BAXTER
Dailey, Irene	LIZ MATTHEWS
Dale, Daniel	MATTHEW CORY
Dana, Leora	SYLVIE KOSLOFF
Dano, Linda	FELICIA GALLANT
Danson, Randy	MISS ROSE
Danziger, Maia	GLENDA TOLAND
D'Arbanville, Patti	CHRISTY CARSON
Darling, Kerri Ann	ALLI FOWLER

Davis, Terry	STACEY WINTHROP
Dawson, Curt	ZACHARY COLTON
Dawson, Vicky	EILEEN SIMPSON
DeBael, Jean	GLORIA NORRIS
DeJesus, Wanda	GOMEZ
Dengel, Roni	SUSAN MATTHEWS
DeVries, John	DINO AMATI
Dewey, Judy	BLAINE EWING
Dewey Carter, John	GRANT TODD
Dion, Colleen	BRETT GARDNER
Dixon, Gail	EMILY MASON
DonHowe, Gwyda	ILSA FREDERICKS
Doran, Jesse	MARIUS SLOAN
Doran, Robert	JAMIE FRAME
Dorn, Franchelle	RITA MADISON
Douglas, James	ELIOT CARRINGTON
Dufour, Val	WALTER CURTIN
Duncan, Carmen	IRIS CARRINGTON WHEELER
Dunne, Richard	DARYLL STEVENS
Dupire, Serge	MICHAUD CHRISTOPHE
Durning, Charles	GIL McGOWAN
Dwyer, Virginia	MARY MATTHEWS
Eda-Young, Barbara	REGINE LINDEMAN
Edson, Hilary	STACEY WINTHROP
Eichhorn, Lisa	ANNIE MERRIMAN
Eplin, Tom	JAKE McKINNON
Espy, William Grey	MITCH BLAKE
Estrin, Patricia	JOAN BARNARD
Evans, Dillon	REGINALD FEARING
Evans Luciano, Judi	PAULINA CORY CARLINO

Ewing, Geoffrey	ADAM BANKS
Fabes, Lindsay	CHARLIE FRAME WINTHROP
Ferguson, Sandra a.k.a. Sandra Reinhardt	AMANDA CORY
Ferrer, José	REUBEN MARINO
Firestone, Scott	WALLY CURTIN
Fitzpatrick, John	WILLIS FRAME
Fletcher, Steve	HANK KENT
Flood, Ann	ROSE LIVINGSTONE
Floyd, Roger	KYLE BARKLEY
Ford, Constance	ADA HOBSON
Ford, Faith	JULIA SHEARER
Ford, Tisha M.	MARY SUE MORGAN
Forsyth, David	JOHN HUDSON
Fowler, Clement	MARTIN CALLAHAN
Frangione, Nancy	CECILE DE POULIGNAC
Franz, Elizabeth	ALMA RUDDER
Frazer, Mark	PRINCE
Freeman, Morgan	ROY BINGHAM
French, Arthur	AL EDWARDS
Fry, Ed	ADAM CORY
Gabet, Sharon	BRITTANY PETERSON LOVE
Gallison, Joseph	BILL MATTHEWS
Galman, Peter	DOUGLAS CARSON
Garfield, Michael	JERRY GROVE
Gari, Roberto	ALISTAIR
Garza, Blaise	GREGORY HUDSON
Gautieri, Christopher	GREGORY HUDSON
Gee, Kevin John	YOSHI ITO
Gentry, Robert	PHILIP LYONS and CRAIG MORRIS

Getz, John	NEIL JOHNSON
Gianese, Rick	RICK GRAHAM
Gibbons, Rob	MEL LAFFERTY
Gibbs, David	BRIAN TIBBS
Gibbs, Timothy	GARY SINCLAIR
Gibson, Robert	ROY BARRY
Gillette, Anita	LORETTA SHEA
Gladstone, Jason	WALLY CURTIN
Going, Joanna	LISA GRADY
Goldin, Ricky Paull	DEAN FRAME
Goodwin, James	KEVIN ANDERSON
Goodwin, Michael	SCOTT BRADLEY
Gould, Gordon	HAYWOOD
Graham, Elain R.	ETTA MAE BURRELL
Grammer, Kelsey	DR. CANARD
Grant, Charles	EVAN FRAME
Grant, Micki	PEGGY HARRIS NOLAN
Green, Brian Lane	SAM FOWLER
Greene, Cathy	SALLY FRAME
Greene, Kim Morgan	NICOLE LOVE
Gregory, Nick	FAIRFAX NEWMAN
Griffith, Thomas Ian	CAITLIN EWING
Griggs, Robyn	MAGGIE CORY
Groom, Sam	RUSS MATTHEWS
Haines, Larry	SIDNEY SUGARMAN
Hall, Troy	TITO BANACEK
Hamilton Dan	JEFF STONE
Hammett, Mike	DENNIS WHEELER
Harmon, Steve	CHRIS TYLER
Harney, Susan	ALICE MATTHEWS

Harper, Ron	TAYLOR HALLOWAY
Harris, Berkeley	BUD PARKER
Harris, Cynthia	RUTH HARRISON
Harris, Harriet	CATHY HARRIS
Harris, Steve Richard	ZAK WILDER
Harry, Jackee	LILY MASON
Harvey, Eric Laray	DARRYL BECKET
Hashim, Edmund	WAYNE ADDISON
Hatch, Eddie Earl	BILLY COOPER
Hawkins, Trish	MIMI HAINES FRAME
Hawthorne, Kimberly	DANA KRAMER
Heche, Anne	VICKY and MARLEY HUDSON
Hedison, David	SPENCER HARRISON
Heineman, Laurie	SHARLENE HUDSON
Hendrickson, Benjamin	SERGEANT BARTLETT
Heyman, Barton	FRED EWING
Hilboldt, Lise	JANET SINGLETON
Hindy, Joseph	BURT McGOWAN
Hinkle, Marin	ALISON VAN ROHAN
Hobart, Deborah	AMY DUDLEY
Hodgen, Morgan	GREGORY HUDSON
Hodges, Patricia	MAISIE WATKINS
Hogan, Robert	VINCE McKINNON
Holbrook, Anna	SHARLENE HUDSON
Holcomb, Tim	JAMIE FRAME
Holder, Christopher	PETER LOVE
Hollen, Rebecca	PEGGY LAZARUS
Holmes, Jered	BRIAN BLAKE
Holzlein, Seth	JAMIE FRAME
Hopkins, Kaitlin	KELSEY HARRISON

Horan, James	DENNY HOBSON
Horton, John	LEONARD BROOKS
Hossack, Allison	OLIVIA MATTHEWS
Hover, Robert	RUSS MATTHEWS
Howard, Anne	NICOLE LOVE
Hudson, Rueben-Santiago	BILLY COOPER
Hughes, Missy	SARA MONTAIGNE
Hughes, Tresa	EMMA ORDWAY
Hurd, Michelle	DANA KRAMER
Huston, Gaye	LEE RANDOLPH
Hutton, John	PETER LOVE
Hyde, James	NEIL JOHANSSEN
Imershein, Deidre	SAMANTHA HOUSTON
Impert, Margaret	RACHEL CORY
Ingram, Jay	CAL ZIMMERMAN
Innes, Laura	NORA DIAMOND
Irby, Dean	MARSHALL LINCOLN KRAMER III
James, Clifton	STRIKER BELLMAN
Janney, Leon	JIM MATTHEWS
Jarkowsky, Andrew	MARK VENABLE
Jefferson, B. J.	RONNIE LAWRENCE
Jenner, Barry	EVAN WEBSTER
Johnston, Lionel	MICHAEL RANDOLPH
Jones, Arthur E.	CLAUDE KELLY
Jones, Christine	JANICE FRAME
Jones, Linda C.	RITA KENT
Jones, Mallory	VENA VENNUCCI
Joyce, Stephen	PAUL CONNELLY
Kalem, Toni	ANGIE PERRINI
Katz, Paul	DOOLEY

Kay, Pamela G.	THOMASINA TODD
Keating, Charles	CARL HUTCHINS
Keats, Steven	ED MCCLAIN
Keith, Lawrence	LEFTY BURNS
Keith, Susan	CECILE DE POULIGNAC
Kelker-Kelly, Robert	SAM FOWLER and SHANE ROBERTS
Keller, Mary Page	SALLY FRAME
Kerr, Elaine	LORETTA SIMPSON
Kerry, Anne	JANET SINGLETON
Kiberd, James	DUSTIN TRENT
King, David	BILLY COOPER
Kinkead, Maeve	ANGIE PERRINI
Kishpaugh, Adam	ALEX CORY
Klaboe, Dana	AMANDA CORY
Knight, Christopher	LEIGH HOBSON
Komoroski, Liliana	DAPHNE GRIMALDI
Korot, Alla	JENNA NORRIS
Kramer, Bert	ALEX WHEELER
Krassenbaum, Mark	JERRY HOCH
Kraus, Philip	BARROWS
Krause, Brian	MATTHEW CORY
Kristen, Ilene	MADELEINE THOMPSON
Kya-Hill, Robert	FRANK CHADWICK
LaGuardia, Michael	CULLEN
Landon Geier, Sofia	JENNIFER THATCHER
Landry, Laurie	NICOLE LOVE
Lange, Jeanne	CAROL LAMONTE
LaRosa, Julius	RENALDO
Lau, Laurence	JAMIE FRAME
Layne, Mary	CHRIS MACALEER

Leak, Jennifer	OLIVE GORDON
Lee, Kaiulani	SHARON AMATI
Leeds, Elissa	HOPE BAUER
Leigh, Janna	JULIA SHEARER
Lemmons, Kasi	TESS
Lenard, Mark	ERNEST GREGORY
LeNoire, Rosetta	GLORIA METCALF
Lewin, Rhonda	VICKY HUDSON
Lewis, Mark Kevin	ANDREW MILLER
Liberatore, Lou	JERRY LOMBARDI
Lien, Jennifer	HANNAH MOORE
Ligon, Tom	BAILEY THOMPSON
Lindley, Audra	LIZ MATTHEWS
Liotta, Ray	JOEY PERRINI
Little, Cleavon	CAPTAIN HANCOCK
Littlefield, John	GARY SINCLAIR
Lochran, Peter	DANIEL GABRIEL
Lohan, Lindsay	ALLI FOWLER
Longley, Mitch	BYRON PIERCE
Love, Darlene	JUDY BURRELL
Luciano, Austin Michael	DANTE CARLINO
Luciano, Melissa	JEANNE EWING
Luisi, James	PHILIP WAINWRIGHT
Lumb, Geoffrey	MITCHELL DRU
Lyles, Leslie	SHERI KENT
Lyman, Dorothy	GWEN PARRISH
Lyman, William	KEN PALMER
Lynde, Janice	TRACEY DEWITT
MacDonald, David Andrew	JORDAN STARK and DAVID HALLIDAY
MacLaren, Jim	DAVID CAMPBELL

Madden, Donald	CURT LANDIS
Maher, Joseph	LEONARD BROOKS
Mahoney-Bennett, Kathleen	SALLY MADISON
Maienczyk, Matthew	MATTHEW CORY
Makris, Jennifer Alexis	ELENA LOPEZ
Malin, Sarah	STEFANIE PRESTON
Malone, Laura	BLAINE EWING
Mansur, Susan	LORETTA DELAHANTY
Marcantel, Christopher	PETE SHEA
Marchand, Nancy	THERESE LAMONTE and MRS. MCCREA
Marie, Kristen	CHERYL MCKINNON
Markel, Danny	SAM FOWLER
Marlowe, Hugh	JIM MATTHEWS
Martin, Marcella	FLO MURRAY
Mascorino, Pierrino	TOM ALBINI
Masters, Ben	VIC STRANG
Mathews, Carmen	BESS KILLWORTH
Matthews, Walter	GERALD DAVIS
Maurice, Christian	MATTHEW CORY
Maxwell, Roberta	BARBARA WEAVER
Mayo Jenkins, Carol	VERA FINLEY
McCabe, Marcia	BUNNY EBERHARDT
McCarthy, Ann	SAMANTHA
McClain, Saundra	JUDY BURRELL
McClanahan, Rue	CAROLINE JOHNSON
McClatchy, Kevin	NICK HUDSON
McConnell, Judith	MIRANDA BISHOP
McCouch, Grayson	MORGAN WINTHROP
McCrossan, Terrence	TRENT FORBES
McDonald, James	BLADE

McDonald, Lora   MARIANNE RANDOLPH
McDonald, Tammy   RUTH HARRISON
McDonell, Allison   EMILY MADDUX
McGinn, Walter   DAVID ROGERS
McGuire, Maeve   ELENA DE POULIGNAC
McKiernan, Dennis   WALLY CURTIN
McKinsey, Beverlee   IRIS CARRINGTON and EMMA FRAME ORDWAY
McMahon, Julian   IAN RAIN
McNulty, Aiden   JAMIE FRAME
McWilliams, Caroline   TRACEY DEWITT
Meacham, Anne   LOUISE GODDARD
Mead, Tyler   JAMIE FRAME
Mendels, Rolanda   MOLLY ORDWAY
Merlin, Joanna   EMILY CORY
Meyer, Taro   MELISSA NEEDHAM
Milgrim, Lynn   SUSAN MATTHEWS
Miller, Betty   JEANNE EWING
Miller, Taylor   SALLY FRAME
Milli, Robert   WAYNE ADDISON
Minor, Michael   ROYAL DUNNING
Mitchell, Ralph Edwin   DASHIEL ST. GEORGE
Mitri, Tiberia   MARIANNE RANDOLPH
Monahan, Kelly   KEN PALMER
Montero, Tony   EDDIE CARLINO
Moor, Bill   JESS COOPER
Moore, Vera   LINDA METCALF
Morran, Jay Huff   VINCE FRAME
Mortimer, Mark   NICK HUDSON
Morton, Joe   ABEL and LEO MARSH
Moss, Laura   AMANDA CORY

Mowry, Lynn	DORIS BENNETT
Munker, Ariane a.k.a. Ariana Chase	MARIANNE RANDOLPH
Murphy, Donna	MORGAN GRAVES
Murphy, Kellyann	CHARLIE FRAME WINTHROP
Murphy, Rosemary	LORETTA FOWLER
Murray, Brian	DAN SHEARER
Nall, Sara	JOYCE CAMPBELL
Nash, John	STEVEN FRAME
Naughton, Greg	PATRICK MILLER
Negro, Mary Joan	ANNE WHITELAW
Neil, Alexandra	EMILY BENSON
Nelson, Johnny	GREGORY HUDSON
Nichols, Josephine	GRANDMA EVANS
Nissen, Tim	MICHAEL RANDOLPH
Norris, Christopher	MARGARET ALLEN
North, Alan	CAPTAIN DELANEY
Norton, Leonie	CINDY CLARK
O'Brien, David	ALAN GLASER
Oehler, Gtretchen	VIVIEN GORROW
O'Keefe, Jodi	MAGGIE CORY
Oliver, David	PERRY HUTCHINS
Oliver, Ralph	CHARLIE RUSHINBERGER
Osburn, Julie	KATHLEEN MCKINNON
Owen, Beverly	PAULA MCCREA
Pacific, Jerry	DR. PRESSMAN
Paeper, Eric	KEVIN JULIAN
Paley, Petronia	QUINN HARDING
Parker, Alexander	MATTHEW CORY
Patterson, Lee	KEVIN COOK

Payton Wright, Pamela	HAZEL PARKER
Peluso, Lisa	LILA ROBERTS
Penberthy, Beverly	PAT MATTHEWS
Pentecost, George	TONY THE TUNA
Perri, Paul	JOEY PERRINI
Peterson, Lenka	MARIE FENTON
Pettiford, Valarie	COURTNEY WALKER
Pfenning, Wesley Ann	ALICE MATTHEWS
Phalen, Robert	ROSS
Philips, Julie	SALLY FRAME
Phillips, Jeff	MATTHEW CORY
Pickens, James Jr.	ZACH EDWARDS
Pickett, Bronson	SCOTT GUTHRIE
Pickles, Christina	ELENA DE POULIGNAC
Pietropinto, Angela	CONNIE CORELLI
Pillar, Gary a.k.a. Gary Carpenter	MIKE BAUER and RAYMOND GORDON
Pinter, Mark	GRANT HARRISON
Ponazecki, Joseph	DAVID THORTON
Ponzini, Antony	DANNY FARGO
Porter, Rick	LARRY EWING
Poston, Francesca	DONNA BECK
Power, Edward	HARRY SHEA
Poyner, Jim	DENNIS WHEELER
Pratt, Lauren	CHARLIE WINTHROP
Preston, James	SCOTT RAYMOND
Prince, Clayton	REUBEN LAWRENCE
Prince, William	KEN BAXTER
Pryor, Nicholas	TOM BAXTER
Rademaker, Connor	KIRKLAND HARRISON

Rademaker, Sean	KIRKLAND HARRISON
Rambo, Dack	GRANT HARRISON
Ratray, Peter	QUENTIN AMES and CHRISTOPHE BOUDREAUX
Reehling, Joyce	LINDA TAGGERT
Reilly, Luke	TED BANCROFT
Reinhardt, Sandra	AMANDA CORY
a.k.a. Sandra Ferguson	
Reinholt, George	STEVE FRAME
Rhames, Ving	CZAJA CARNEK
Rhodes, Kim	CINDY BROOKE HARRISON
Rich, Christopher	SANDY CORY
Rich, Katie	DEE EVANS
Richard, Trevor	KEVIN THATCHER
Rivera, Teresa Sofia	LUISA RIVERA
Roark, Caitlin	MAGGIE CORY
Roberts, Eric A.	TED BANCROFT
Robinson, Chris	JASON FRAME
Rodell, Barbara	LEE RANDOLPH
Rodrick, Michael	CAMERON SINCLAIR
Roerick, William	RICHARD GAVIN
Rogers, Cory Lee	TOMMY KENT
Rolfing, Tom	CLIFF TANNER
Rollins, Howard E. Jr.	ED HARDING
Ross Kendrick, Rhonda	TONI BURRELL
Roux, Carol	MISSY PALMER
Ruger, Loriann	MARIANNE RANDOLPH
Ruger, Tom	MICHAEL RANDOLPH
Runyeon, Frank	ED MCCLAIN
Runyon, Jennifer	SALLY FRAME
Russ, William	BURT MCGOWAN

Russek, David Lee	CHIP RAYBURN
Russom, Leon	WILLIS FRAME
Ryan, Michael M.	JOHN RANDOLPH
Ryland, Jack	VINCE MCKINNON
Sabota, Tom Jr.	MICHAEL RANDOLPH
Salem, Dahlia	SOFIA CARLINO
Salisbury, Colgate	DAVID THORTON
Sampler, Philece	DONNA LOVE
Santigo-Hudson, Ruben	BILLY COOPER
Sanz, Carlos	VICTOR RODRIGUEZ
Saxon, John	EDWARD GERARD
Scardino, Don	CHRIS CHAPIN
Schmidtke, Ned	GREG BARNARD
Schnetzer, Stephen	CASS WINTHROP
Schrink, Nicole	MAGGIE CORY
Scollay, Fred J.	CHARLEY HOBSON
Scott, Hillary	ALLI FOWLER
Secrest, Jim	ANDY CUMMINGS
Sedgewick, Robert	HUNTER BRADSHAW
Sedgwick, Kyra	JULIA SHEARER
Seitz, John	ZACK HILL
Serrano, Diego	TOMAS RIVERA
Sexton, Dee Ann	CINDY LEE
Shackelford, Ted	RAYMOND GORDON
Shaler, Anna	PHYLLIS
Sharon, Fran	SUSAN MATTHEWS
Sharp, Jonathon	SERGEI RADZINSKY
Shay, Michelle	HENRIETTA MORGAN
Shelton, Sloane	LORETTA DELAHANTY
Sheridan, Ann	KATHERINE CORNING

Siebert, Charles	DR. PHILBIN
Simmons, Henry	TYRONE MONTGOMERY
Simon, Joel	RUDY ENRIGHT
Siravo, Joseph	BARRY DENTON
Sisler, Craig	ALAN LEWIS
Sloan, Tina	OLIVIA DELANEY
Small, Peggy	CLARA HUDSON
Smith, Lois	ELLA FITZ
Smythe, Marcus	PETER LOVE
Snyder, Drew	SAM EGAN
Sones, Pat	HILDA
Spencer, Sally	M. J. MCKINNON
Spencer, Sheila	THOMASINA TODD
Steen, Richard	BEN MCKINNON
Stenborg, Helen	HELGA LINDEMAN
Stenovitch, Nadine	JOSIE WATTS
Sterling, Phil	RAFE CARTER
Sternhagen, Frances	JANE OVERSTREET
Stevens, Paul	BRIAN BANCROFT
Stewart, Francelle	RITA MADISON
Stone, Michael	CRAIG CALDWELL
Strasser, Robin	RACHEL CORY
Stroud, Duke	VINCE MCKINNON
Strudwick, Shepperd	JIM MATTHEWS
Stuart, Anna	DONNA LOVE
Stuart, Eric Morgan	CHRIS MADISON
Sullivan, Dennis	MICHAEL RANDOLPH
Sullivan, John	MICHAEL RANDOLPH
Sullivan, Jude	GREGORY HUDSON
Sullivan, Susan	LENORE MOORE CURTIN

Sutton, Lon	DICK NOLAN
Sweet, Dolph	GIL MCGOWAN
Swope, Tracy Brooks	CHRISTINE WYLIE
Sykes, Kim	JUDY BURRELL
Templeton, Tony	TITO BANACEK
Teresa, Mary	LILA DAWSON
Thatcher, Kristine	MISS STEINER
Thompson, Victoria	JANICE FRAME
Tillinger, John	LEONARD BROOKS
Timmins, Cali	PAULINA CORY
Tinder, Paul	JERRY GROVE
Todd, Russell	JAMIE FRAME
Toll, Pamela	PAMMY DAVIS
Tomlin, Gary	MORGAN SIMPSON
Toner, Thomas	HORACE BAKEWELL
Torsiglieri, Anne	SUSAN WELLER
Tovatt, Patrick	ZANE LINDQUIST
Trageser, Kathy	BLAIR BAKER
Trent, Joey	RUSS MATTHEWS
Tribbey, Vana	ALICE MATTHEWS
Trustman, Susan	PAT MATTHEWS
Tucci, Christine	AMANDA CORY
Tulley, Paul	SCOTT BRADLEY
Turnbull, Jill	MARIANNE RANDOLPH
Turner, Janine	PATRICIA KIRKLAND
Valley, Paul Michael	RYAN HARRISON
Vernoff, Kaili	LAURIE MICHAELS
Walker, Kathryn	BARBARA WEAVER
Wallace, Adrienne	MARIANNE RANDOLPH
Ward, Janet	BELLE CLARK

Wasilewski, Paul	SEAN MCKINNON
Watson, Douglass	MAC CORY
Wedgeworth, Ann	LAHOMA VANE LUCAS
Weston, Ellen	KAREN GREGORY
Wheeler, Ellen	VICKY and MARLEY HUDSON
White, Bridget	BLAIR BAKER
White, Persia	KC BURRELL
Whitfield, Dondre	JESSE LAWRENCE
Wickwire, Nancy	LIZ MATTHEWS
Widdoes, Kathleen	ROSE PERRINI
Wiggin, Tom	GIL FENTON
Wilkinson, Kate	CLARA HUDSON and MRS. FRANKLIN
Willey, Walt	JIM LARUSSO
Williams, Billy Dee	ASSISTANT DISTRICT ATTORNEY
Williams, Murial	HELEN MOORE
Willis, Alicia Leigh	ALLI FOWLER
Wilson, Alexandra	JOSIE WATTS
Wilson, Kristen	LILA DAWSON
Wilson, Pasean	DANA KRAMER
Wilson, Tara	JULIE ANN EDWARDS
Wolfe, Karin	PAM SLOANE
Woods, Eric Scott	EVAN FRAME
Wright Holmes, Prudence	ANNIE MERRIMAN
Wyndham, Victoria	RACHEL CORY and JUSTINE DUVALIER
Yates, Stephen	JAMIE FRAME and CHRIS PIERSON
Young, Bellamy	COURTNEY EVANS
Young, Janis	BERNICE ROBINSON
Zachar, Glen	MICHAEL RANDOLPH
Zimerle, Thom	RICK GRAHAM
Zorich, Louis	MILO SIMONELLI

Answers to Quizzes

All about Rachel

1. (b) Gerald; 2. (b) model; 3. (a) at Steve and Alice's engagement party; 4. (a) a ring Mac had given Rachel; 5. (b) Mitch Blake; 6. (c) in a collapsed building; 7. (b) She was left blind; 8. (a) red; 9. (b) She needed his stock to prevent a corporate takeover; 10. (d) Cory and Elizabeth

Aliases—Criminal and Otherwise

1. (c) Fanny Grady; 2. (a) Mac Cory; 3. (c) Steve Frame; 4. (c) The Vulture; 5. (a) Earl; 6. (b) Kate Baker; 7. (b) Joy Lamont; 8. (d) Hadley Prescott; 9. (b) Marnie; 10. (a) David Halliday

Here Comes the Bride

1. (a) first; 2. (b) in her parents' living room; 3. (c) That he had bribed Rachel's father to commit perjury during the custody battle for Jamie; 4. (a) her twin sister, Vicky; 5. (a) at the race track; 6. (b) Venice; 7. (a) the fifth anniversary of Mac's death; 8. (b) He colored all over it; 9. (c) The Harbor Club had been shut down as a health hazard; 10. (a) Cass Winthrop and Gary Sinclair

From Hollywood to Bay City

1. (b) *Bronco Billy*; 2. (a) Lisa Peluso (LILA ROBERTS CORY); 3. (b) *A Summer Place*; 4. (a) *The Fly*; 5. (b) *The Godfather Part II*; 6. (c) The Mel Gibson–Danny Glover *Lethal Weapon* buddy films; 7. (b) Jason Voorhies in *Friday the 13th Part II*; 8. (c) John Considine (VIC HASTINGS and REGINALD LOVE); 9. (a) Kale Browne (MICHAEL HUDSON); 10. (b) *The Bodyguard*; Bonus: (a) Augusta Dabney (LAURA BAXTER)

Long Night's Journey into Day

1. (b) *Bonanza*; 2. (c) Timothy Gibbs (GARY SINCLAIR); 3. (d) *Voyage to the Bottom of the Sea*; 4. (a) *Dallas*; 5. (c) *Knots Landing*; 6. (d) Ricky Paull Goldin (DEAN FRAME); 7. (d) *Wiseguy*; 8. (d) *Trapper John, M.D.*; 9. (c) James Douglas (ELIOT CARRINGTON); 10. (d) Christopher Knight (PETER); Bonus: (c) Cindy

Nice to See You Again

1. (a) Emma; 2. (c) Danny Markel; 3. (d) Vic Strang; 4. (a) Dr. Alton Spader; 5. (c) a groupie; 6. (a) writer; 7. (d) Lucas Castigliano; 8. (d) Ted Shackelford (GARY EWING, *Knots Landing*); 9. (b) Robert Gentry; 10. (b) 6

Just Passing through Town

1. (c) "Chopsticks"; 2. (c) a magician; 3. (a) Sally Jessy Raphael; 4. (b) Virginia Graham; 5. (a) Al Roker; 6. (c) José Ferrer; 7. (c) Peabo Bryson; 8. (b) Emma Ordway; 9. (c) She was Grant's public relations expert; 10. (b) Betty White

Another Quiz

1964. (a) New York; 1965. (a) She came down with pneumonia; 1966. (c) Missy learned that she was illegitimate; 1967. (b) Lahoma Vane; 1968. (d) LSD; 1969. (a) He was killed in a boating accident; 1970. (b) Wayne lied that Lenore had been sleeping with him; 1971. (c) Caroline Johnson; 1972. (c) She fell off a stepladder; 1973. (a) Alice Matthews; 1974. (b) bribing Rachel's father to commit perjury during Jamie's custody trial; 1975. (a) Australia; 1976. (c) She took an overdose of sleeping pills; 1977. (a) Her husband Gil was killed in an explosion; 1978. (d) the pump house; 1979. (a) Iris wanted to break up the relationship between Dennis and Cecile's mother; 1980. (c) It left him sterile; 1981. (b) Blaine Ewing; 1982. (b) kidnapping his son Matthew; 1983. (c) to research her next novel; 1984. (b) Tanquir; 1985. (d) the designer drug Ecstasy; 1986. (c) in a car crash; 1987. (b) John Hudson; 1988. (a) a kitchen table in the Frame farmhouse; 1989. (d) all three women; 1990. (b) horse; 1991. (b) New Orleans; 1992. (a) Ace Records; 1993. (a) rape; 1994. (d) manic depression; 1995. (a) Jake McKinnon; 1996. (b) The governor pardoned Grant after he saved his daughter's life during a fire; 1997. (b) handwriting; 1998. (d) *Embers in the Snow*; 1999. (c) Lumina; Bonus. (b) 9,000

Bibliography

Bonderoff, Jason. *Soap Opera Babylon*. New York: Perigree Books, 1987.

Groves, Seli. *Soaps: A Pictorial History of America's Daytime Dramas*. Chicago: Contemporary Books, Inc., 1983.

Holly, Ellen. *One Life: The Autobiography of an African American Actress*. New York, Tokyo, and London: Kodansha International, 1996.

Hyatt, Wesley. *The Encyclopedia of Daytime Television*. New York: Billboard Books, 1997.

LaGuardia, Robert. *Soap World*. New York: Arbor House, 1983.

Lemay, Harding. *Eight Years in Another World*. New York: Atheneum, 1981.

McNeil, Alex. *Total Television: A Comprehensive Guide to Programming from 1948 to the Present*, 4th edition. New York: Penguin, 1996.

Meyers, Richard. *The Illustrated Soap Opera Companion*. New York: Drake Publishers, 1977.

Nash, Bruce and Allan Zullo. *The Hollywood Walk of Shame*. Kansas City, MO: Nash & Zullo Productions, Inc., 1993.

O'Neil, Thomas. *The Emmys: Star Wars, Showdowns and the Supreme Test of TV's Best*. New York: Penguin, 1992.

Rout, Nancy E., Ellen Buckley, and Barney M. Rout (editors). *The Soap Opera Book: Who's Who in Daytime Drama*. West Nyack, NY: Todd Publications, 1992.

Schemering, Christopher. *The Soap Opera Encyclopedia,* 2nd edition. New York: Ballantine, 1987.

Waggett, Gerard J. *The Soap Opera Book of Lists.* New York: HarperCollins, 1996.

————. *The Soap Opera Encyclopedia.* New York: HarperCollins, 1997.

My research also relied on back issues of *Soap Opera Weekly, Soap Opera Digest, Soap Opera Magazine, Soap Opera News, Soaps In Depth, Soap Opera Update,* and *TV Guide*.

Index

About the Author

GERARD J. WAGGETT is a leading expert on soap operas. He is the author of *The Ultimate Days of Our Lives Trivia Book* (Renaissance, 1999), *The Soap Opera Encyclopedia*, *The Soap Opera Book of Lists*, *The Official General Hospital Trivia Book*, *The As the World Turns Quiz Book*, *The Official All My Children Trivia Book*, and *The Soap Opera Puzzle Book*. He has written about daytime television for *Soap Opera Weekly*, *Soap Opera Update*, and *TV Guide*. He is a graduate of Harvard College and holds a master's degree in English from the University of Massachusetts.

also available from
RENAISSANCE BOOKS

The Ultimate Days of Our Lives Trivia Book
BY GERARD J. WAGGETT
ISBN: 1-58063-049-9 • $9.95

Soap Stars to Superstars: Celebrities Who Started Out in Daytime Drama
BY ANNETTE D'AGOSTINO
ISBN: 1-58063-075-8 • $14.95

Party of Five: The Unofficial Companion
BY BRENDA SCOTT ROYCE
ISBN: 1-58063-000-6 • $14.95

That Lawyer Girl: An Unauthorized Guide to Ally's World
BY A. C. BECK
ISBN: 1-58063-044-8 • $14.95

Matt Damon: An Unauthorized Biography
BY CHRIS NICKSON
ISBN: 1-58063-072-3 • $16.95

and coming soon . . .

Daytime Divas: The Grand Dames of Soap Operas
BY KATHLEEN TRACY
ISBN: 1-58063-087-1 • $14.95

TO ORDER PLEASE CALL
1-800-452-5589